Direct Marketing

A STEP-BY-STEP GUIDE TO EFFECTIVE PLANNING AND TARGETING

RODDY MULLIN

IN ASSOCIATION WITH
Marketing

KOGAN PAGE

First published in 2002

Kogan Page Limited
120 Pentonville Road
London N1 9JN
UK

Kogan Page US
22 Broad Street
Milford CT 06460
USA

© Roddy Mullin, 2002

British Library Cataloguing in Publication Data

A CIP record for this book is available from the British Library.

ISBN 0 7494 3677 8

Typeset by Jean Cussons Typesetting, Diss, Norfolk
Printed and bound in Great Britain by Clays Ltd, St Ives plc

Contents

Preface

BACKGROUND

If the rise and rise of direct marketing bewilders you, you are not alone. Even seasoned marketers, surveys show, are finding the same difficulty in keeping up with direct marketing, alongside the new media, the new technologies, accountability and the changing needs/demands of customers. The customer can now view so much when deciding to buy, just how does a customer choose what to buy? How do marketers get their own concept – product/service – in front of the customer?

Direct marketing is often the best answer – understand it, use it and customers will flock in. This book explains and shows you how to carry out direct marketing, to help you use it to persuade customers to choose to buy from you. The real plus of direct marketing is 'the message you send' is 'the message received'. A look at the customer at the end of 2001 finds:

▓ The customer is bedazzled by choice and often looks for the brain-relieving, easy option, to save having to make too many decisions in this time-dominated complex world of choice. The ultimate example of this is that the customer is now choosing to bond with a brand, if it is possible and appropriate, buying from just one supplier, not bothering even to look at competitors. You are fortunate if it is your brand. If not, you have a real challenge.

■ The customer expects individual, consistent attention and respect – entirely suited to direct marketing – which is why direct marketing is beginning to dominate marketing as other marketers discover this. So, in a kind of way, you have no option but to carry out direct marketing to keep customers, to find more customers and to stay in business.

■ The customer moreover, research shows, requires businesses to integrate operations, showing a seamless perspective to them, removing any vertical separations of marketing, sales, set up and service. The firms that resist – and there are many – will not survive. Integration in any case, research shows, can raise sales by 30 per cent. If you don't integrate your business by applying internal marketing, and assuming your competitors do; then, expect to fail.

■ Customers expect real customer relations to be in place. Customer relations that are found to be merely a sop to fob off complaints will no longer work. Banks are probably most at risk here. A survey showed that only HSBC (including First Direct) had hardly any complaints. Customers expect honest answers. If none are forthcoming, customers will move their custom.

So, in this plethora of bewilderment, what can a marketer, or anyone contemplating taking on marketing, do? In time-honoured Douglas Adams fashion – DON'T PANIC. This book helps you find the answers. In practice, most answers to most marketing requirements can be met through direct marketing – once you have customers listed – and a way is suggested here to overcome the lack of a list too.

This is a 'how to' book. That is, it explains when to use and how to carry out, or manage others carrying out, direct marketing. The subject is approached in a no-nonsense, and what used to be called a 'user-friendly', way. Hopefully it follows logically, from the start point of business objectives and 'purpose' through to achievement; that is, having delivered direct marketing activities you can prove they are value for money.

Direct marketing is a UK growth industry, increasing by 22 per cent over the last two years (as at September 2001) to a £10.1 billion annual activity. The Direct Marketing Association's (DMA's) Chairman, Jenny Moseley, forecasts that in many areas it will prove to be the superior method over former 'above-the-line' marketing (advertising and PR etc), directly communicating with existing and potential customers.

To put direct marketing into the perspective of its component parts, *direct mail* is a £2.1 billion a year business; *direct response advertising* for magazines and posters is about £1.9 billion (out of £9.4 billion spent on all press and poster advertising) and TV and radio is about £1.8 billion (out of £5.2 billion spent on all TV and radio advertising); while *telemarketing* stands at £2.4 billion. The *new media* (Internet, mostly) is at £158 million (all of it direct marketing). So direct marketing is more than half (at 59 per cent) of the total spend on all UK marketing activities of £17 billion. Clearly, many people believe that direct marketing is now superior. (source: DMA/AA). See the figures at the end of Chapter 1.

Looking at it another way, what might be the reason for this direct marketing interest? In the UK, the customer has access to 283 TV channels, 292 radio stations, 8,500 magazines and over 2 million Web sites. This fragmentation can be the despair of anyone trying to find where their prospective customers are looking, listening or reading. But such despair might also be true of the customer – looking for specific help to satisfy a need and so many places to look. The Internet with its search engines is not necessarily the answer. The Economist Intelligence Unit quotes that 97.4 per cent of information on the Web is invisible to search engines. Recent research (summer 2001) shows that people go on to the Internet to satisfy a specific task – not just to browse. Searching, not surfing is actually what happens. This suggests that you need to drive traffic to Web sites – a task for direct response – giving the customer a specific purpose first. Equally, you can drive the traffic to mail order or catalogues or to a retail chain.

Once you have found each other – customer and company – then the onus is on the company to take the initiative to build the relationship. Once you have attracted your customer to you, you need to build the belief and trust of your customer in your concept – your product/service. Customers follow a buying process, which they vary depending on the concept – the product or service – they seek. You have to match that buying process with a sales process and take account of the influencers on which the customers rely. The *brand* is the shorthand mental picture held in the mind of the customer and contains the values of the brand that relate to the satisfying of a need. In a busy world this is powerful stuff and with constant reinforcement, people now bond to a brand as a convenient and easy way to satisfy a need without making the brain examine the competitor alternatives each time, unless a brand fails them. Direct marketing is totally suited to the building of relationships.

Another future scenario predicts that high value customers will choose to use multi channels with any firm or organization to communicate and transact business with them; that is, they may go on the Internet, make a telephone call or pay a personal visit to an outlet. In retail banking, multi channel users are 25–50 per cent more profitable than single channel users. Multi channel users also reduce the 'cost per revenue £' by up to 15 per cent. Direct marketing covers all the channels.

Consideration is given in this book to when direct marketing itself is of primary strategic importance. Direct marketing used to be considered as the second class option (the 'below the line' description did not help) and hence as a subsequent or lower priority marketing activity. In the past it has been considered only after the 'more glamorous' advertising and PR. Direct marketing activity is now recognized as a key activity that can sometimes be the best business strategy to achieve marketing objectives arising from business objectives. The growth of new technologies in breadth and depth provides sophisticated means to find and communicate with potential clients and enables access to elusive customers, without wastage. Beware of traditional agencies that tell you to stick to just advertising or just PR – they are dinosaurs.

This book is written specifically about direct marketing, but within an integrated marketing approach. Integration is now recognized as important for marketers, particularly as part of the process of building customer brand bonding, which has to be carried out in a consistent fashion.

Recent research (July 2001) is showing that a failure to be consistent can cause a substantial loss of sales; that is, customers reject the sale within their statutory rights period when presented with differing messages – by 'marketing', by sales, by those in 'set up' if appropriate where a customer opens their account – and, early on in the relationship, by 'after sales service'. Achievement of integration and consistency is through internal marketing.

ABOUT THE BOOK

The book itself is structured in the following way:

■ The treatment of the subject tries to match the need to be able to pick up a subject quickly following a logical reader/customer need to build up an understanding of each direct marketing activity. This is achieved by describing, in a consistent way, each activity, what it can do, what purpose it can achieve, when to apply it, and how to do it, how to set and measure success, along with a few tips.

■ The book covers the new media – where direct marketing is now possible; both via e-mail and the permission-based mobile Internet.

■ Useful tips and examples are included in a framed box in most chapters.

■ A bit of the history of direct marketing is in Appendix 2 along with many facts and figures (updated to mid-2001) should you need to be persuaded of the rise of direct marketing by historic facts.

■ Measuring direct marketing activities and their success is given some coverage in this book. This follows the principles given in another Kogan Page title, *Value for Money Marketing*, also by the author. That book gives a fuller understanding of the reasoning behind the need to measure marketing activities and benefits that accrue from setting key performance indicators – the criteria for success – and comparing the results.

Other good books approach the subject of direct marketing from different perspectives:

■ To obtain an understanding and feel for direct marketing the fourth edition of Drayton Bird's *Commonsense Direct Marketing* is a lovely readable book.

■ Judith Donovan's *DIY Direct Marketing* book cover describes itself 'as an essential guide for beginners'. It is just what it says on the cover.

■ This book says what should be included in a letter without giving examples; these examples can be found in Drayton Bird's *How to Write Letters that Sell*, Kogan Page.

Scope and purpose

The scope of this book is to allow a reader to encompass an under-standing of and encourage a greater application of direct marketing activities. Hopefully you may find a few blinding flashes of the obvious. For example the envelope in which you place a mailing does matter – just think of how you size up a letter before you open it and mentally prepare yourself for what is inside. When you are about to make a telephone call, do you think of the person at the other end? You should. If you see on the data-base a person is over 60 – pause before you initially speak to them; they are of a generation that did not use first names and the person you are calling may prefer a title, Mr or Mrs or Miss, etc rather than a first name as given in the database. This is important, as the grey market grows in both size and importance – there are more of them, they have money and they have the time to spend it.

Much of what you need to know about direct marketing is here. Inevitably, someone will have added something new before this goes to print. One essential thing is guaranteed not to be provided by the book. The missing ingredient is the enthusiasm provided by the individual marketer for the use and application of direct communication as a marketing activity. This is where you come in and hopefully the reading of this book will provide the enthusi-astic inspiration.

To instil a 'bit of passion' into the reader for direct marketing is a part of the purpose of this book. Charles Handy sees passion as a key requirement of success both in life and in business. He is right. The contents of this book aim to give the reader the confidence and understanding to make decisions about direct marketing activities and how to include them in an integrated marketing plan (to achieve marketing objectives). The book provides the knowledge, describes the skill and understanding required to enable the reader to implement marketing activities individually or manage and control the direct marketing activities of others.

Remember, the real plus of direct marketing is 'the message you send' is 'the message received'. There is no channel or media or other interference to misinterpret or distort it. It is one-to-one. Yes, to avoid the 'gatekeepers' you may need a ruse or two – included in this book as tips – but with direct marketing there is a fair chance that the messages you want to get to the recipient will do just that. So you must get the messages and the delivery right.

After three chapters on the application of direct marketing, the book describes each of the direct marketing activities available in Chapters 4 to 13 thus:

▓ the marketing activity on its own – what it is and what it can and cannot achieve;
▓ its strategic role as a marketing activity that is part of an integrated marketing approach to the marketing communications mix;
▓ how to make it happen, along with descriptions of associated topics, not strictly direct marketing;
▓ possible measures of achievement and how such achievement is measured;
▓ the practical use of and tips for each of the direct marketing activities – in a frame;
▓ where you can find an idea of the likely cost (Royal Mail and others provide these on Web sites, etc);
▓ pointers to any regulations, codes of practice, the law etc.

The direct marketing activities themselves and associated topics considered in the book – a chapter on each – are given in the list of contents. Not covered in the book are advertising and PR; the direct marketing focus of the book removes consideration of advertising and PR. (Other books in the Kogan Page series consider both.) The book also does not cover the basic writing of copy or basic layout of print. This again is covered in software and in print elsewhere.

Achievement

For the marketing practitioner this book supplies the tools, within the context of a business plan and its business objectives and the forming of marketing objectives, to give (strategic) consideration as to when it is appropriate to use direct marketing activity to achieve those marketing objectives. When you have read this book, you should be able to communicate confidently and directly with your customer using direct marketing activities.

If the book has challenged you the reader into thinking more about when and how to use direct marketing and inspired you with more enthusiasm for direct marketing, then that too is an achievement, a bonus, a plus. As with the author's previous book, feedback about this book's usefulness is welcomed by both the author and Kogan Page.

What is direct marketing?

DEFINITION

Direct marketing is a communication between seller and buyer directly. No intermediary media is used. No distractions come between – hopefully. Direct marketing is generally visual and sometimes auditory. It is also, to an extent sensual and olfactory. That is, impressions are obtained from feel and smell that affect the communication. It is direct communication but with a marketing purpose. It is most often in text format. Layout and delivery (both the form and the timing) have an impact on the acceptability of the communication. Research shows that a combination of brochure and Internet works, persuading people to buy – the Internet needs the brochure's reassuring feel and existence, giving an Internet site substance.

Other authors have defined direct marketing. Drayton Bird (2000) describes it as 'an advertising activity, which creates and exploits a direct relationship between you and your prospect or customer as an individual'.

Judith Donovan's (2000) definition of direct marketing is that it is 'the science of arresting the human intelligence long enough to take money off it'.

The Direct Marketing Association (DMA) defines direct marketing as 'communications where data are used systematically to achieve quantifiable marketing objectives and where direct contact is made, or invited, between a company and its customers and prospective customers'.

Margaret Allen, in the Kogan Page book preceding this one, did not feel the DMA definition really covered the benefits direct marketing can bring. She used the words 'one-to-one communication' and 'to keep open a dialogue that is vital in long-term relationship-building'. This suggests a campaign rather than the tighter definition below, which allows for a single activity. In this book, the need to consider the customer's perceptions and language is recognized. This book also puts a dampener on excessive creativity, which is outside the scope of the customer to perceive. This puts the focus back on a marketing purpose, rather than just 'art' marketing to win industry awards at the client's and customer's expense.

This book defines direct marketing as 'the delivery of a marketing message or proposition to a target customer or potential customer, in a customer-favourable format, put to the customer from the seller or the seller's agents (including call centres) without an intermediary person or indirect media involved'.

Throughout this book hereafter the 'potential customer' is subsumed in the word customer. Let's hope it saves a few trees. A customer makes the purchase and is either or both, a consumer or a (business) client.

STARTING WITH THE CUSTOMER – THE ESSENTIAL KNOWLEDGE

Why do you need to start with the customer? The days of customers buying what they are offered are gone. The customer has an amazing amount of choice – your task is to persuade them to really want to buy from you and again and again. Remember, customers are affected by their background, their social or cultural influences; they consider and think of matters in different ways; they have varied economic purchasing power; their intelligence varies; they have prejudices.

Identifying your customer

Clearly you need to understand your customer – whoever that is – whether they are an existing customer or a potential customer. You need to find out all about them to serve them better, retain their custom and persuade them to buy more. Everyone in your organization needs to know about them. Equally, the customer will be finding out about your company or organization. It is a two-way communication. In finding out about your customer and they finding out about you, you will establish a relationship. Making sure you do that well and that the customer trusts your firm is called customer relationship management (CRM). You should 'aim to provide a consistent customer experience wherever the customer touches you each time'.

Identifying your customer and establishing a customer profile – an idealized, averaged, but complete understanding of the way the customer thinks, what the customer is influenced by, how, when, what and from whom they are prepared to buy – is really important to grasp, as without customers you make no sales. With no sales a business dies. Marketing is tasked with identifying and knowing the customer. If you discover that there is more than one common type of customer, each with a different approach to buying from you, you have discovered segments. Each of the different, yet identifiable, separate customer groups is known as a segment. Sorting all types of customers by segments is called market segmentation. Market segmentation is only helpful where each segment has a different approach to buying and a size, purchasing power, accessibility and future viability, from which you will make a profit.

If you are selling to buyers and the buyers are selling on your product or service to customers who are consumers, marketing will need to understand both tiers of customers – that is, the primary buyers and the primary buyers' own buyers or consumers. If you are dealing with business-to-business (B2B) customers, their customers too may be business customers. There are differences within each tier. You need to know and understand them all.

So now the different types of customer have been roughly separated into segments, how do we store all the information and keep it all in mind just in case they call? What you need to understand about customers is not an infinite amount of detail – though some database systems supplied for customer relationship management can now offer this facility. What you need to know is the information about the customer that is relevant to making a sale or relevant to you at that moment, in that part of the sales process. You need to have that knowledge in front of you only when the customer is in front of you or is on the telephone to you. This is called knowledge management – the provision of timely and relevant information at the moment you need it – more of this later. Recognizing that even a seemingly simple customer overview is quite complex to analyse is helpful to an understanding of marketing.

Think from the customer viewpoint

People end up with so much baggage from the culture and social environment of their upbringing, their education, their life experience, it is easy to make assumptions about how others think and are likely to respond to communications with them. Accept the fact; the people you are selling to are unlikely to be from the same cultural, social, educational, life experience background as yourself. Take this fact as really important. If not, you may have a problem grasping the need for marketing and the rest of this book.

It is easy to assume that one target group of customers is a segment much like another and despite research for which you may have paid, in real life, your own people (even perhaps yourself) have been found to ignore that research and apply what they have done before – because it's easy, because it's easy to plead that it worked before, because... and everyone has such convincing reasons for doing what you have always done and forgetting the research. Don't ignore it; believe and act on your market research.

For every customer segment that you decide to select as a target (you do not need to target every segment), just before you start analysing the target customer apply the following method:

▨ Erase from your mind your own thinking and prejudices.
▨ Learn to listen, observe and grasp how your target thinks, communicates, comes to conclusions.
▨ Understand what makes the target tick, react, etc.

This method has been described as self-recognition criteria – accepting that the way you think and react is certainly wrong for any target you are analysing. You should not make any assumptions about the target customer. Find out.

Now that an open mind exists about the customer, let's do just that; find out and consider what makes them tick and how they express their needs.

The customer expectation

This involves giving great consideration to the following five points:

- ▓ *The basics.* The whole concept you are offering as a supplier and from the customer perspective, must match what they need, want and perceive to be the solution to their need, offering greater benefit – ie an advantage – over other suppliers. The description should consider the six Cs – more below. You should describe your concept in their language using their perceptions.
- ▓ *Branding.* This is the process of achieving occupation of a piece of the customer's mind to remind them you exist as and when they need you. It is a powerful thing a successful brand and when you achieve brand bonding... the world is your oyster, or rather and more importantly, you will sell a lot.
- ▓ *Buying process.* That is, understanding that the customer adopts a buying process, different for different purchases and you have the task of finding out what it is and developing a sales process to match. Research shows that many first stage Internet sites forget the need to match the way their customers buy.
- ▓ *Building relationships.* People are people and like to build a relationship, you just have to accept this. If a person gives you inconsistent answers you trust them less. This is also true of customers making contact with different parts of an organization. Integration means making sure every part of your business delivers consistent answers. Research shows it is worth 30 per cent of sales (or a loss of 30 per cent if you do not practise it). How you achieve full integration practically is through internal marketing.

■ *The role of influencers.* Others influence customers when making purchases and this influence must be understood. You need to know how those around the customer, the people they follow and their perceived status can influence their buying behaviour. Remember, you can use people who embody influence, a public figure, a personality, to endorse your product or service. Public figures do on occasion fall, so take care when making your selection.

The five points above are explained in more detail below. They have an impact on all marketing activities. The specific impact on each direct marketing activity is covered in later chapters.

The basics: expressing and delivering what you are offering from the customer perspective
Organizationally-based marketing traditionally considers the needs of the customer in terms of four Ps:

■ the product or service;
■ the place;
■ the price;
■ the promotion.

Note: others do add Ps for process, people and physical evidence to make the list seven Ps. This approach gives the wrong perspective for the marketing needs analysis of the customer in the 21st century and the subsequent decision making about which marketing activities to apply. It is better to approach the customers' (whether buyer or consumer) needs *in terms of their view* of the four Ps.

Actually, what you are really doing is applying self-recognition criteria – looking at the Ps – from the customer view. And when you do this, the four Ps become six Cs (this is not new, it is an extension of Philip Kotler's preferred viewpoint):

■ *Cost.* A customer considers cost (and cost of ownership as part of that consideration). A customer also puts into the equation the cost in terms of both time expended and actual cost of travel to make a purchase. The Future Foundation research indicates that consumers will travel for most of their activities and purchases within a 14-mile radius of their home.

▓ *Convenience of buying.* A mix of place/location, opening hours, cash/cheque/credit card acceptability. Customers are lazy – exercising the brain requires effort and energy – so make it easy for them.

▓ *Concept.* A mix of product and service – few products are sold without some sort of aftercare service. The quality and fitness for purpose of the concept are assumed to be right. A warranty or return policy is taken for granted. A brand is a consolidation of the concept into an easy-to-remember space in the mind of the customer.

▓ *Communication.* How well the product or service is communicated to them. Customers will not buy if it is too complex or does not put the concept across in terms they commonly use. This explains why some advertising fails.

▓ *Customer relationship.* That formed between customer and the seller – CRM (customer relationship management) principles apply – the customer expects to be treated with respect at all times and that all reasonable questions will be answered. Once they have made a purchase of any size or have signed up for a service, they expect to be recognized as a customer (for example once a customer has had a car serviced at a garage a customer rightfully expects the garage to know all their car's idiosyncrasies when they call). That expectation includes the resolution of all problems relating to that concept which they purchased from you and their perceived status as your customer.

▓ *Consistency.* The reassurance of ongoing quality and reliability of the other five Cs – brand surety if you like. It comes from the application of integration of marketing through the application of internal marketing.

This book considers the customer viewpoint hereafter in terms of the six Cs.

Understanding how branding works for a customer
The effect of branding on the customer is very powerful if the branding is done properly. You need to create a favourable and appropriate perception and image about your company and its products/services – the concept you are offering – ideally so that the customer thinks that their perception of your firm's product/service provides the answer at the moment that need

occurs in the customer's mind. The development of ownership of a part of a person's mind is called brand creation. The deeper that brand is fixed is called brand bonding. When a person buys only your brand you have ultimate success.

Customers are attracted to a 'concept' usually by their perception of the corporate brand. Customers retain perceptions and images, and their own key senses trigger a brand if the retention has been successful. It is a 'shorthand' memory device, a mix of logo, slogan or a feeling, which the customer relates to 'advantage' with regard to a need. If you have such recall in a customer, you are made. But beware, if the concept you are selling does not match the perception and image and experience of the customer, you are far less likely to make a sale.

It is quite possible to have different perceptions of your brand in different parts of the globe or even in different parts of the same country. Guinness advertised for a time in Africa, unwittingly using a symbol that meant that Guinness improved fertility. Brylcream was thought to be a food delicacy in another African country. A failure of branding may not be a disaster if the concept sells and you are happy to sell with that branding mismatch.

It is also quite possible to reposition a brand. Sometimes this is essential to save a brand that has become dusty and failing. Failures are often the seedcorn of success if the lesson is understood. Lucozade was re-branded as a sports drink from its previous life as an expensive drink for when you were ill.

An example of how successful branding works

Imagine a picture frame about an arm's length in front of and slightly above your head. Hold your hands out and pretend to hold opposite corners. (Just do it – you won't look too mad.) The picture frame is blank until something fills it. Consider it as an extension of your mind.

Now let us test your brand perceptions. If you are told 'Coca Cola', what image flashes into the imaginary picture frame? A particular bottle shape? The word 'refreshing'?

How about 'IBM'. Perhaps your imaginary picture frame is now filled with a word/logo or image of a computer? (Research among lecture audiences shows most people put 'computer' into their picture frame.)

Assuming that you too thought IBM equals 'computer', is that a good thing for IBM. Well, no, actually. As that is not what IBM is selling nowadays. IBM is now selling 'business solutions'. IBM used to sell just computers – so the brand perception fails in terms of being beneficial to sales. IBM should consider giving IBM as a name, to a computer firm and re-naming itself something like 'Big Blue Solutions'.

Let us try the perceptions the other way round. What appears in your imaginary picture frame if we say 'Blackcurrant'. If you are in the UK, is it 'Robinsons' or 'Ribena'? This is where your selection may reflect your exposure to the media they use. But if you chose one or the other, they are in luck; you will probably head for their product as a preference, if you need to purchase blackcurrant. You have developed a bonding to a brand.

Use the same picture frame technique on 'Lever Brothers'. Here a firm has chosen to go for product branding rather than a corporate brand. You may not associate any products immediately with Lever Brothers. Your picture frame remains empty. Actually, Persil is one of their products. Persil is very well known. But when they introduce changes to the product, they have a problem. Using a different name would be difficult and expensive to promote to reach the existing Persil sales levels. So they use additional words – 'new', 'improved', 'non-biological' – to retain the product brand association. To keep the bond with the brand.

Does your company name appear in your customers' picture frames? If yes, you have a successful brand. If not, you may need to call in a marketer. If you don't know if you have a successful brand, a marketer will find out through customer research then suggest the remedial measures so that your name does appear in your customers' picture frames – and you can measure that achievement through more research.

If brand association is instantly there and you have retained it in your customers' heads, it is a powerful sales supporter when the customer sets out to purchase. Analysts are beginning to recognize and measure this brand bonding power as an intangible asset. It is a better long-term indicator of a firm's success than the financial trend picture. It is a CEO deliverable.

How did the perception and image of a brand get there – the brand that you conjure up in your imaginary picture frame? It is a carefully considered process of effective marketing activity, probably involving drip-feed promotion over a long period of time. Equally, it is possible to destroy a brand if it is not policed. To achieve a brand may not actually cost a lot. A programme of marketing activity is required, covering in an integrated way all aspects of the business operation and marketing communications – advertising, PR, direct mail, and so on.

Hopefully, the power of branding for a customer has now been demonstrated. You can achieve it for your firm. You set a business vision, which requires a particular image and perception – a brand – among your customers. From that is constructed a marketing objective to achieve effective branding. Whether you have 10 or 10,000 or 10 million customers, the task is to get your brand – a name or a logo (think of McDonald's 'M') or a mix of the two and all the associated perceptions and images – into their heads, for ready summons into the frame.

How does the customer buy?

The buying process

The customer follows a buying process, which needs to be analysed and understood, and a sales process then needs to be developed (by marketing) to match it. If it is a two-tier market then two analyses and two solutions will be required to understand how you sell to the customer; one solution prepared for the buyer, one solution prepared for the consumer. If the tiers are themselves divided into segments then additional analyses and solutions will be required and for different sales environments.

Every customer as a buyer approaches purchasing of products/services (the concept) in a considered way and it muddles the customer if their buying process is not followed. Customers have different buying processes for different 'concept' purchases. For the same concept purchase, different customers will each have a separate buying process. For example, when food shopping, commodity item purchasing is carried out in an almost impulse fashion with brand recognition foremost; as opposed to the consideration given to a speciality food item when a more detailed examination and comparison of alternative items on offer takes place. When the same customer sets off to buy a sofa or car they use more input from intermediaries – friends, family, journalists, commentators – and the effect on their own image is also considered.

The feedback of information from the customer about perceptions, wants and needs, which started in the earlier stage when creating the conducive environment, provides the message content and direct marketing activity then allows a bespoke marketing proposition to be prepared and delivered in a preferred format and at a preferred time.

Assume there is a point at which a customer has a blank mind – an empty picture frame. Into that blank appears a need, which, as has been described, can be rapidly associated with a brand. If that occurs and purchase of the brand satisfies the need the process stops. The mind may however not think of a brand or may indeed feel the desire to seek an alternative if bonding to a brand is not strong, or by way of variety or change, the mind may decide deliberately to ignore a brand.

Once a need is established then the buying process begins. For example, a life partner may say 'we need a new sofa and two armchairs'. Suppose no brand occurs in the 'picture frame' for a sofa and two armchairs set; the mind then seeks alternatives such as the word 'furniture'. Assume a number of furniture outlets appear – DFS, Courts, Ikea, Arding & Hobbs and the like. All have promoted their brands and related them to 'furniture'.

What then happens? Thinking begins and a discussion may start, trying to *specify*, *define* and *identify* the parameters of the sofa and two armchairs set required. Note that some people, without inspiration or imagination, may well action the next stage – a search – and then carry out the first stage. The specifying, defining and identifying process may consider any, a number, or all of the following:

▦ the material;
▦ the size;
▦ should the sofa convert into a bed;
▦ the colour;
▦ the design;
▦ the price range that is acceptable;
▦ if the set has a warranty;
▦ the make;
▦ whether to buy the set through some finance arrangement;
▦ any additional cost of delivery, or whether delivery is free.

Friends and relatives are likely to be consulted or will offer opinions. These influencers can seriously affect the specification and their input and influence are considered in a later paragraph.

Next a *search* for a sofa and two armchairs takes place. This could start on the Internet or on a TV shopping channel or by examining brochures at home (Ikea etc), but consumers generally like to experience goods of this type – so visits take place. A number of local furniture shops, department stores, warehouse specialists will be visited – probably the ones that appeared in the 'picture frame' under 'furniture'. It is unlikely that any decision will be made to buy the first sofa and two armchairs seen. This kind of purchase is not an impulse buy.

Evaluation and selection occur from the moment the first sofa and two armchairs set has been seen. Some sets will be rejected as not meeting the specification, other sets will be identified as being of an unacceptable quality, wrong aesthetic shape and so on. The influence of the salesperson can be significant by throwing in additional points of specification usually related to positive points about a set he or she is keen to sell.

Once a decision to buy has been reached the actual purchase takes place. Even at this moment a number of causes can delay or stop purchase. The process may require signature of a contract and acceptance of a complex form in small writing of terms and conditions, which can stop a purchase. The acceptability of the means of payment may stop or delay the transaction. Until fairly recently, Marks & Spencer and John Lewis did not accept credit cards. Problems may arise with financial loan or hire purchase arrangements, which may cause the customer to walk away. The speed of processing the purchase transaction may be important to the customer. A long queue in prospect or an unfriendly sales assistant may cause a customer to walk out.

The buying process does not stop at the purchase. A customer will monitor the performance and operation of the purchased product or service. Unsatisfactory aspects may cause the seeking of redress in money terms or some other form of compensation. The legal rights pertaining to purchases and the warranty period may apply. If the monitoring proves beneficial, the customer will log the experience either to influence others interested in purchasing the product or service or for a repeat future purchase.

The sales process

The sales process is achieved by matching the buying process, applying the six Cs and ensuring the operation is easy and customer-friendly. Forming a sales process is a marketing activity. The table below outlines the buying and sales processes:

Table 1.1　*Establishing the sales process from the buying process and buyer needs*

Buying process

Buyer needs	Perfect response	Practical procedures
Identify, define, specify	Matches six Cs	Find out needs – match six Cs, qualify, check buyer proposition, relevance, performance
Search	Fully aware of product/services and benefits at the right moment = sell advantage	Market benefits, offer advantage; potential customer contact – knows where to look confirmed, build relationship
Evaluate and select	Be helpful, reiterate	Give yardsticks, sell
Purchase	Unthreatening Easy to say yes to	Clear, if any, contract terms, convenient
Monitor	All positive	Feedback Build relationship towards next purchase

From the buying process of the customer, you match with a sales process for the sales staff.

Sales process

Point in process	Objectives	Practical steps
Just become aware of	Build relationship, fact find, qualify, do not try to close a sale	Deliver evidence of six Cs, ask questions

Aware but not a customer	Obtain a sales opportunity – test close	Keep in contact Contact plan Put across matched benefits
Sales opportunity	Win sale	Find buyer detail needs – match six Cs benefits Try closing
Now a customer	Demonstrate correct purchase occurred	Feedback on performance

Building relationships
Customers react more favourably when there is confidence in an organization and they have some form of redress through a relationship developed over time. The brand building may provide this to an extent. The consumer receives this purchase confidence initially from the warranty, the guarantee that is backed by legislation.

The importance of establishing links between businesses
In business-to-business the warranty is often not enough. You should always consider establishing links at different levels of the business with your customer. It can be described as the 'rubber glove' theory. Interlock fingers between firms (the gloves) at all levels within the firm (the fingers) and make sure he links are difficult to separate (the rubber). It may happen anyway, particularly with service firms – but do not leave it to chance.

The principle is simple. At each appropriate level you should make sure a link is established. This should not just be encouraged or left to chance. It must be an instruction. When a contract is signed then agree and decide the need for more links. People should be nominated at director, manager, supervisor, even delivery and shop floor level.

In a very small firm, make sure another director or partner is involved. This would normally be the senior partner or managing director for clients of other directors. In a solicitor's department the partner in charge of the department should make contact with all the clients whose matters are being worked on by fee earners in the department. Just one phone call is enough to establish links. Forming links and maintaining them – using a contact plan – is a marketing activity.

Building relationships for repeat sales

The need to build relationships is important and should be encouraged. For relatively small effort, a large number of repeat sales can be made. Make contact with those who have bought before in a timely fashion. A car dealer should ascertain the buying period between new car purchases of customers – often from historic data. Then as the time when a purchase becomes imminent, information about new cars, offers to view, invitations to test drive should be forthcoming. This is often the opposite of reality – when a person is inundated with mail just after a purchase but by the time a new purchase is about to be made – nothing is communicated. Building relationships is a marketing activity.

It is important to establish re-order frequency and match a contact call to that period. For a professional firm seeking new business it is even possible to ask how frequently contact should be made. It can be made into a process with a contact plan for each client. That is, people in the team are tasked with maintaining contact at set frequencies and the type of contact decided. The process can be managed centrally using a database.

The part played by the influencer
Buyers, when they make buying decisions, are influenced by their positions within their own business environments, their social environment and their status in society. They worry about the attitudes of others to the decision they take: of their superiors, peers, subordinates, friends and family, to a greater or lesser extent. Marketing must seek and identify these influencers, add them to the knowledge management process and satisfy the buyer's needs using that understanding. In some cases, using a celebrity to endorse the concept provides a focus as the influencer.

Business buyers have a complex relationship with their influencers in a firm unless they are the owner. This introduces the possibility of many different people influencing the buyer and the buying decision that is made. Buyers are influenced by:

- ■ where the buyer is in the hierarchy of the firm;
- ■ how the buyer fits in within the firm;
- ■ to whom the buyer reports;
- ■ the office politics/culture/relationships.

Such information is readily stored on a computer database.

FITTING DIRECT MARKETING INTO THE INTEGRATED MARKETING ENVIRONMENT

Marketing purpose

Direct marketing is no different from other forms of marketing in that it is trying to achieve a marketing purpose. The marketing purpose is to meet a marketing objective; the direct marketing activities may be in support of other marketing activities or as one of a sequence of direct marketing activities – often called a campaign. Direct marketing achieves the purpose directly. The fact that direct marketing is a one-to-one communication allows the communication to be special and tailored to the recipient. If you do not use its special characteristics and its individual capability, you are missing a trick and the true benefit of direct marketing.

The old business-orientated way of operating marketing

In marketing, in the last decades of the 20th century, the basic marketing effort was managed as a three-part exercise for the benefit of the business, often by separate operations, first trying to generate leads (the old marketing bit), secondly to process sales (the task of the sales force to close sales) and finally to retain the customer (the domain of customer service).

Separation of the three parts no longer really works. However carefully people are told to join together as a team to support a customer, if they belong to different parts of a business they are likely to retain in-house rivalries. It is a human condition. Integration means working as one, probably achievable only under one leader.

An integrated marketer is aware of four factors: the recent customer research on consistency of message (the customer shies away from purchase if the message is inconsistent); the discerning nature of customers, reflecting a greater maturity; the customer only believing messages that are supported by reality; finally, the pace of life itself is moving customers to bond with a brand that delivers what they need because they do not have the time to waste re-examining the marketplace every time they make a repeat purchase. (Tesco is the consumer model here with 43 per cent of their high value customers 100 per cent bonded to the brand – that is, they do not shop anywhere else. Viking is an equivalent good example on the business-to-business side.)

The wise marketer now looks at the whole approach from product and service (concept) awareness to demonstrating relevance and performance, to showing clear advantage of the concept and finally bonding, that is, from the viewpoint of the customer, creating a seamless consistent view, which persuades the customer not to even consider or think of buying from anyone else.

The newer integrated marketing purpose

The marketing purpose for an integrated marketer must be the whole approach of the customer seen from the customer's viewpoint. That is:

▓ *The creation of a sales-conducive environment both real and virtual (that is, in the mind)* to create an environment that is conducive to sales and repeat sales through building a relationship with a customer that:
  - takes account of the customer's particular needs including awareness of the product/service (the concept) and showing the relevance and performance to the customer of 'the concept';
  - educates the customer from whatever level they wish to start and;
  - discovers, then communicates messages in ways that match the customer's understanding;
  - makes it all easy to remember for the customer, by associating everything the customer needs to know with a brand, which is placed in the mind (as a kind of shorthand memory need-matcher).

The blinding flash of the obvious here is that to achieve this successfully (assuming you are not going to dedicate a marketing person to each customer, which, of course, happened in the past and is still done now for really big clients using key account managers) you are going to have to build up a database for everyone to access, informing 'on-call' everything you need to know about the customer, in your relationship with them. It also means obtaining feedback to build up the picture of the customer (what used to be called fact finding). The opportunity to determine whether a sale is likely or not can also be undertaken so time is not wasted on an unlikely prospect (what used to be called qualifying the customer).

The benefit of direct marketing being used to achieve this sales conducive environment is that for awareness and education, complex propositions can be put across most easily in print and considered at a pace that suits the potential customer. For feedback similarly, the completion of a questionnaire can be carried out at a pace that suits the potential customer. The same applies to a telemarketing or a call centre call (where the call person can both start to build a relationship and ensure that the potential customer understands the concept) or receiving information over the Internet (with extensive Frequently Asked Questions [FAQs] supplied) and completing an e-mail response. In every case the feedback of information allows subsequently an enhanced capability to produce bespoke propositions to send back to potential customers. The brand values are fed in through everything.

▪ *The delivery of an advantageous marketing proposition* to put forward a marketing proposition. This is a proposal somehow conveying advantage – it may be information about special purchasing opportunities, it may be an entreaty to purchase. It is, however, entirely persuasive and conducive to a customer's purchase.

The marketing proposition meets the needs of the customer – communicated from their perspective, best expressed by the six Cs. It also uses a sales process that matches the buying process preferred by the customer.

Two blinding flashes of the obvious here. First the six Cs are the marketing mix elements but seen from the customer viewpoint – cost, convenience, communication, customer relations, concept and consistency. The marketer implants this information as favourable and complete messages in the mind of the customer in a form that is customer digestible. Second the buying process has to be discovered and the sales process then designed and matched to it.

■ *The customer bonding with the brand* to increase a customer bond with a brand, by imparting specific messages that strengthen that bond and building long-term relationships for repeat or further sales.

Customers, if approached correctly, bond in a way that is much stronger than any loyalty scheme. It requires continuing confirmation of the excellence of the customer decision to bond and must continue to demonstrate advantage. The result, if achieved though, is repeat purchase and ongoing business. This bonding is so effective it is now being used as a measure of future share value prediction. It is in consequence a CEO deliverable. Again direct marketing is particularly suited to achieve customer bonding with a brand. It will often require more than one direct marketing activity – a campaign – over a period of time.

The need to build relationships is important. Building relationships is a marketing activity and direct marketing is the superior implementation method for this. For relatively small effort, a large number of repeat sales can be achieved. Direct marketing is good at cementing relationships with customers to achieve sales. In business-to-business where costs of advertising in the specialist press seem profligate and in any case marketing budgets are more limited and seeming wastage is unwelcome, direct marketing is an ideal tool. Indeed customers can be readily persuaded to share in the saving of cost by ordering online and allowing automated systems to cut out the usual business interfaces – intermediary persons, firms or organizations. Airline and some rail ticketing can and now do save on cost for consumers.

It is particularly important to make contact with those who have bought before, both in an appropriate and a timely fashion. It is important to establish re-order frequency and match a contact call or letter to that period. Some advocate a 90-day period between contacts. This is no longer subtle enough.

From experience, a buying pattern can be established. Customers can even be asked how frequently they want to be contacted; for a professional firm seeking new business it is even possible to ask how frequently contact should be made. It can then be made into a process with a contact plan for each client. That is, persons in the team are tasked with maintaining contact at set frequencies and the type of that contact decided. The process can be managed centrally using a database. For example, the car dealer mentioned before, should ascertain the buying period between car purchases of customers – even asking the customer to say when they had previous cars and for how long. The period in between purchases should build a relationship – perhaps seeking assistance with new product development, finding out the customer preference and demonstrating how the new products will meet those preferences. Then in the pre-purchase period, really putting forward the sell, based on the knowledge of the customer.

Regulations, statutes, codes of practice and the law

As in all business activities there are rules and regulations to follow. Some are voluntary but it is unwise not to comply. There are also statutory bodies and laws, which have to be obeyed. Key items are:

■ The Data Protection Act – a significant piece of legislation. See Appendix 3 for further information. For example, from 24 October 2001 you may not disclose an e-mail address to third parties without permission.
■ The Advertising Standards Authority (ASA) exercises control of printed advertising content the ITC does the same for TV advertising. See Appendix 3 for further information.
■ The Direct Marketing Association (DMA) operates codes of conduct with its members. Non-members are advised to follow them – they make common sense. As a first point of call, the DMA should be able to provide the answers to any immediate query. See Appendix for further information.

JUST HOW EXTENSIVE IS DIRECT MARKETING?

To give an idea of how much is spent on each part of marketing communications and how that has changed over the years, comparison of direct marketing with advertising spend (outdoor, cinema, TV, radio) is given in Figures 1.1, 1.2 and 1.3 below. Comparisons and other facts and figures about who is spending what on what are given in Appendix 2. Clearly direct marketing is a major part of the communications mix.

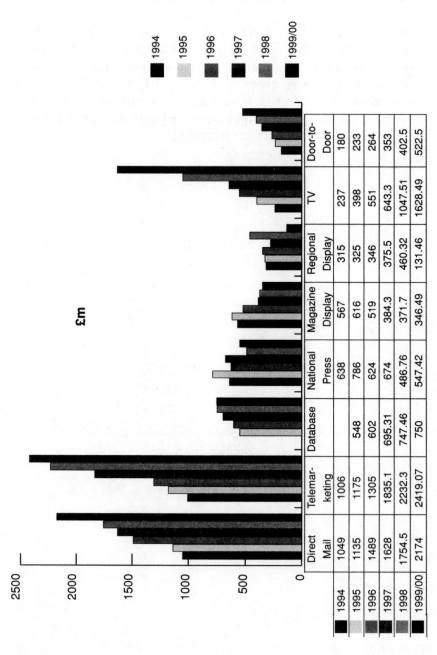

	1994	1995	1996	1997	1998	1999/00
Direct Mail	1049	1135	1489	1628	1754.5	2174
Telemarketing	1006	1175	1305	1835.1	2232.3	2419.07
Database		548	602	695.31	747.46	750
National Press	638	786	624	674	486.76	547.42
Magazine Display	567	616	519	384.3	371.7	346.49
Regional Display	315	325	346	375.5	460.32	131.46
TV	237	398	551	643.3	1047.51	1628.49
Door-to-Door	180	233	264	353	402.5	522.5

Figure 1.1 *Expenditure trends by medium (1)*

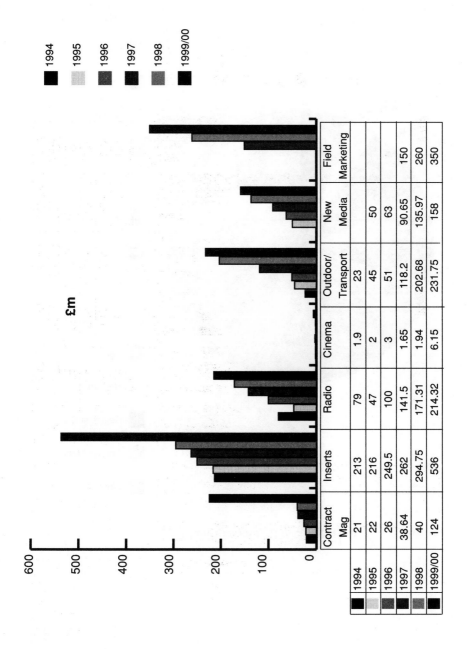

Figure 1.2 *Expenditure trends by medium (2)*

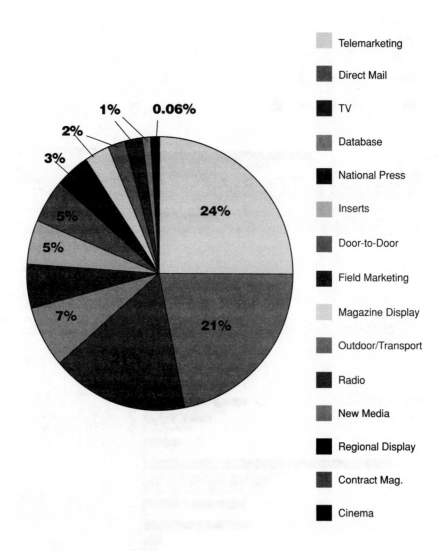

Figure 1.3 *Expenditure share by medium*

2

When to use direct marketing

DECIDING WHEN DIRECT MARKETING IS MOST APPROPRIATE

Direct marketing is most appropriate in a number of situations. The following paragraphs list some of these and, of course, the reverse where direct marketing is inappropriate.

Obtaining a list of customers for direct mail or telemarketing activities

First, there is some obvious logic (blinding flash of the obvious): to carry out some direct marketing activities (eg e-mail, direct mail, catalogue) you need to know your customers by name and address, or e-mail address or telephone number. Only if you have customers can you carry out those direct marketing activities. But if you do not have those customers, then you do have the following direct marketing alternatives:

▓ *Advertise for customers.* Carry out direct response marketing activities first (see Chapter 6), to achieve sufficient numbers of customers' details to carry out direct marketing as part of a campaign. Make the ones you want an offer they cannot refuse. Of course, you do not necessarily want the whole population, so it must be targeted. (For example, Jaguar offering an X-type for the weekend if you leave your BMW or Mercedes with them, thus targeting the wealthy 30+ age group.)

Non-direct response advertising can produce customers but may well be much slower, as you require the customer to take action unprompted and unless your advertising persuades and/or makes an incredible offer that has customers putting in effort to seek out purchase outlets, a lot of potential customers may not bite.

■ *Use PR.* This is probably riskier than non-direct response advertising as you do not control the channel. You could use some high profile concept (product/service) launch that captures sufficient media interest for journalists, commentators and editors to publish and promote your concept. Beware, they may do so, but not always in ways you can imagine.

■ *Buy potential customer names.* Technically, you hire the names for each time you use the list, which comes in a database format. The database, the list, needs to match the profile of your target. Legally, you need to ensure that the database is properly used – that the customers listed have sanctioned your communicating with them on this topic.

■ *Non-names direct marketing.* The direct marketing activities that do not depend on knowing the customers' names, addresses, etc, are: direct response (inserts, tip ons, pop ups), piggy back, door-to-door, leaflets and handouts, all of which are covered in later chapters.

■ *Field marketing.* Field marketing encompasses face-to-face direct marketing (see Chapter 13). Generally this is a relatively expensive form of direct marketing as you are paying for people's time to undertake direct marketing and they are usually only in contact with one or a few customers at any time.

Start-ups

As a start-up business you do not have any customers, so why not use someone else's? Piggy back may offer the perfect solution, providing you select the right partner who has lots of the right type of customers. So just after you have arrived and set up in an area and do not know the locals, pick a piggy back partner who has customers with a concept that has an affinity with yours. More of this in Chapter 8.

Commodity products
Clearly for an item in general use such as a commodity (cosmetic/personal hygiene, food, cleaning materials) you do not need a name and address and door-to-door (see Chapter 9) is an easy and cheap way of delivering a marketing message to households. It is quite possible to target households fairly accurately by the type of persons living there. A number of organizations offer profiles of household types by area or street. A commodity cannot yet be sent over TV or radio or poster, though you can stick on samples to other printed media.

Complex propositions
Direct marketing is comfortable with complex propositions. You cannot deliver the small print in a TV advertisement or a poster or even really in a press advertisement (where the amount of reading is less suited to newsprint than in a printed brochure). Also, financial services are a personal matter suited to direct mail, which is a one-to-one medium, versus a newspaper, which is impersonal.

The recognized uses for direct marketing
Drayton Bird (2000) considers there are five major activities that can be applied singly, in stages or over time, which develop a relationship for direct marketing to persuade the recipient to:

■ buy through the post;
■ ask for catalogues;
■ request a demonstration;
■ visit a retail establishment;
■ take part in some action.

STILL UNSURE WHETHER TO USE DIRECT MARKETING?

Ask some questions

What questions need to be asked and answered before deciding to use direct marketing? Judith Donovan (2000) insists the start point for direct marketing must be a series of questions:

Question	Answer
Whom am I trying to reach?	A specific target; that is what direct mail is good at.
What do I want them to do?	See Drayton's list above.
Why should they do it?	Give clear six Cs customer benefits.
Where should I reach them?	The area – are you tying in the direct mail with TV ads?
When should I reach them?	Midweek for business, weekend for consumers.

She also advocates that the key database information fields for each customer should be recency, frequency, value and product.

The response to direct marketing can be enhanced with a truly exclusive offer – treatment like a VIP, requiring an RSVP, the offer of a gift that is out of the ordinary.

Is a campaign – including direct marketing – necessary?

It all sounds so difficult. Do you really have to have a campaign and what skills do you need? What is this database? Direct marketing may well be one of several associated marketing activities forming a campaign. Several direct marketing activities on their own may themselves be carried out in sequence to achieve a result.

Accepting that a customer operates a buying process, assuming that the six Cs have to be put across for awareness, relevance and performance before clearly showing advantage, then it is probably necessary to assume that this can only be done with a campaign. Would you buy, on the evidence of a single piece of paper, one incoming call, one e-mail? If you wouldn't, why should you expect your customers to be any different? It is possible to use a single piece of paper – try offering a £5 note to every response received – but it is unlikely to bring results (besides you would have to post that £5 to them in a second mailing).

If influencers are important to a customer then some form of indirect marketing activity will be required – such as PR or advertising – to persuade the influencer.

So, the answer is that a campaign is likely to be necessary. Put simply: *a campaign matches the way people buy.*

The importance of appropriate creativity and copy

The skills you should employ are the ability to listen and to observe customers. You do not need degrees in creativity or English literature. Thinking from a customer perspective should limit creativity to what is appropriate – associating messages with your purpose and the brand – within the limit of your customers' understanding. Creativity must be applied intelligently, within that understanding. The message in your copy must match and achieve your purpose. Good copy can draw attention, build conviction and draw on the power of emotion.

An excellent way to find out your customers' perspective is to carry out market research. Employ a market research agency if you are finding out about consumers. If your customer numbers are small or likely to be small (say up to 500 for example in a business) use a marketing consultant to carry out the research. Insist on seeing the questions and the verbatim responses. They will give you examples of the language your customer uses – then use it yourself.

For a time in the last decade of the 20th century it was fashionable to go beyond the understanding of customers and a number of meaningless, messageless (for the customer) advertisements appeared. Do not fall into that trap. When in doubt test advertisements; in fact, always test advertisements on some of your customers.

Testing copy is essential but it is not always done, implies Drayton Bird, who believes in the maxim that you should not change copy until you have found something better.

Database use

All a database is is a compilation of lots of bits of information, which can be sorted in as many ways as the separate bits of information you hold. In this way you can find a single customer rapidly from their name, telephone number, car registration, account number, whatever and then ask the database for all the information about that customer. This is known as accessing the database. Not really very difficult, but an essential tool nowadays for anyone in marketing. It means you can see at a glance everything you have recorded about the customer. If it's not there and you need it, add it to the database. Chapter 4 has a longer description of lists and databases.

3

How to decide which direct marketing activities to use

UNDERSTANDING MEDIA AND CHANNEL TECHNOLOGY

Before deciding the appropriate media channel for your message, gaining an understanding of the alternative technology can be daunting. It is not easy to explain the alternatives in a book. Firms do offer excellent sample CD ROMs and videos free. DVA, a firm offering total media supply services offers free booklets, a video, a CD ROM of examples of alternative Web sites and a Web site to visit, to help understand the technology. Concise, another firm, offers a CD ROM – also free on application. See Appendix 3 for both. Mention this book when calling.

The original technology problems are gradually being overcome. Whereas video on the Web used to have to be downloaded as a complete clip before viewing, it is now possible to download a screen and then download only the changes as they occur. As far as the viewer is concerned, all that is important is that the images appear in enough frequency to fool the eyes. A further problem is the state of the equipment used by the customer – it needs to be of a certain capability. Not much you can do here? Well, you can offer alternative formats for more basic equipment. You can research the likely equipment used by the customer. Video encoding technologies (MPEG1, MPEG2, AVI, QuickTime, RealPlayer, MediaPlayer) are outside the scope of this book to describe. See the DVA booklet for more information. Plug-ins, which are software packages that allow a customer to view the video in whatever format they are provided, should be included in the CD ROM or DVD package you are sending out. DVA provides a CD ROM, which shows the different format and possibilities.

Go digital. DVD offers the smooth transition between video, animation and interactive screens. The need to integrate marketing across all channels, suggests it is best to make the original source material digital. That then allows translation and exploitation into all other media including print, the Internet, videos, CDs, TV advertisements, DVDs, etc.

There are other books in the Kogan Page Marketing in Action series to help with advertising and PR as communication channels, and books on creativity. Further books are planned to cover all the remaining aspects needed to carry out marketing in a business or organization. See Appendix 3 for titles.

GETTING THE APPROPRIATE MARKETING MIX

Produce a marketing plan

The marketing mix you select is your marketing plan. You get there by going through a process of preparing a business plan first. Marketing provides some of the strategic inputs to help decide those business objectives. Once objectives are cleared then you can draw out marketing objectives and look at all the options in the marketing mix (a very large list) before picking those that you believe suit you and will achieve your objectives. The picking process (communication channel planning) is helped by using a customer perspective, both for existing customers and prospects at all times and thinking throughout of 'the six Cs, the buying process of your customers, your brand and their influencers'. The process is really helped if you have an understanding of the technology (see above).

Examples of marketing mix

An example given by Royal Mail is Virgin Money Ltd, which has tested its marketing mix thoroughly in a constant refinement for cost and effectiveness efficiency. This has led to an approximate budget allocation of 35 per cent press and 35 per cent broadcast (direct response), 15 per cent direct mail (with a 3–7 per cent response to mailings) and 15 per cent online (total £8 million spend overall). Awareness of Virgin Money Ltd rose in the first year from 0 to 51 per cent.

Another Royal Mail example is Welcome Holidays with a turnover of £25 million, which, through press, direct mail and online advertising, directs customers to a Web site that allows customers to see where they are going. Welcome Holidays have an internal database from which it mails a brochure to 165,000 previous customers (in August and, for those who have not booked, again in December) and each year a new enquiries database of 125,000 is set up, whom it also mails. The mix typically produces a 3.8 per cent sales conversion (30 per cent up on previous years) and this has produced a 5:1 return on investment with an average cost per sale of £20.

Overcome the easy-life tendency
The process of drawing up a marketing plan is a useful discipline, for if you find activities that have no purpose towards achieving your objectives, then discard them. They are often put in because someone found it too easy to repeat last time's plan – beware the lazy approach.

A Willott Kingston Smith survey (October 2001) found marketers relied too much on agencies to do the decision making for them on media channel selection. The consequence is that the media channels selected change little year on year. If an advertising agency is the sole supplier, beware; a number of agencies are traditionalists who have always made their money from press, poster and TV advertising. Their creative people do not have direct marketing or Web sites 'on their radar'. So unless you insist on the inclusion of consideration of direct marketing with them you may not really get any. The survey uncovered a view that most agencies only really pay lip service to communication channel planning. The way to overcome this is to insist on it or change to an agency that does. Tempus Partners is a new media buying agency, which not only starts with a communication channel plan, but also accepts part of its fees based on success of the channel selection. The survey found a media buyer view that most marketers are incapable of any accountability. Do not be one of them.

The author believes it is essential to measure the success of achievement of the final list of activities you select for your plan. Allocate responsibility for each activity and objective. With the person responsible for each marketing activity, set a key performance indicator (KPI) for their marketing activity. Record the KPI and then measure it. The results indicate the successes or failures of the marketing activities to allow you to make changes next time – and/or allow you to select new marketing personnel! (This is covered in detail in another Kogan Page book entitled *Value for Money Marketing* (Mullin, 2001), from which, incidentally, the planning example given on the following page is taken.).

Planning is essential to achieve focus and control cost. It is a human weakness to write plans then leave them in some filing cabinet. A very short document or table is all that is required and if it is on display, it will trigger the conscience. It is only the marketing activities that will achieve the objectives, true, but it is all too easy to forget what you originally set out to do. A plan allows you to allocate priorities in case a round of cost cuts means a number of activities fall by the way. It will also keep a record of what you cut and how that affected the outcome when the day of reckoning comes. Equally, if the plan succeeds and the KPI is achieved you can praise and celebrate. You also have real quantified experience for next time.

This book is not about how to write business plans or marketing plans but to explain direct marketing activities and how they can be used as part of your marketing mix. The paragraphs and table that follow are purely to illustrate the business process and show how direct marketing channels are selected as part of the marketing plan.

Illustrative business objectives

The final SMART (S = Specific, M = Measurable, A = Agreed, R = Reasonable, T = Timebound) business objectives of a company in sports/leisure cleared by the board and in a priority order might be to:

Table 3.1 *Illustrative marketing plan*

Marketing activity	Person responsible	What is success? The key performance indicator and its metric	Measurement mechanism	Cost of activity and measure	Value for money achieved	Mechanism works?	Future use of activity/ mechanism
Marketing objectives							
To achieve the sales targets set for the year		Achieve the £ figure set	Sales figures – by month, by area, by customer, for year				
To grow the customer database by 40 long-term customers by the end of this year		40 new customers matching the profile of existing customers	Customer database figures – check match of new with old (completed questionnaire, verify and status checks)				
To install the new media – Internet and interactive TV – within six months		Successfully installed Web site and TV commercial made – interactive TV time booked	Observation				
To raise the profile (using an agreed list of measures) to be higher at the end of the year than your direct competitor		Profile is higher on all measures listed (list agreed by board) Measure mid-year to check on position as well as year end	Check recent market research, if not suited re-commission Market research at mid- and end of year after the exhibition				
To operate a stand at the main exhibition		Presence to support profile achievement Budget yet to be agreed	Observation Scope for high visibility activity				

To increase awareness to above 80%, for those active in the sport, of the purpose of the firm and an understanding of the products/services	>80% of those questioned respond favourably Questionnaire to be agreed with the board	Market research after the exhibition – combine with profile-raising research							
Marketing activities									
Mail shots to customers and potential customers	3% response from potential customers (telemarket anyone not responding – see next activity)	Coded responses allow tracking – record totals of mail shots and telemarketing							
Telemarketing potential customers	10% response from potential customers (including mail shot)	Use call logs plus customer database record							
Extranet ordering	Ordering by all Web-enabled customers	Compare database of e-mail customers with orders							
Extranet sales promotions	Sales growth with profit > promotion cost and by all Web-enabled customers	Track responses and orders/offer taken up of database							
Web site ordering by consumers	Shows growth across all areas (persuades non e-mail customers to go on Web)	Track order placing through to customer link							
Call centre ordering by consumers	Shows growth across all areas	Call centre log, track coded responses to customers							

Marketing activity	Person responsible	What is success? The key performance indicator and its metric	Measurement mechanism	Cost of activity and measure	Value for money achieved	Mechanism works?	Future use of activity/ mechanism
Main exhibition acceptances from potential customers		10% response and attend (nil responses telemarketing)	Track coded responses				
Produce a Web site		With 50% repeat visitors	Track site visitors, record repeat visitors				
High visibility activity at main exhibition		An exhibition stopper Budget figure negotiate nearer time	Observation				
PR for high visibility activity		Coverage in a number of national newspapers, articles by commentators and sports journalists in magazines and local papers, radio and TV sports?	Measure scc/display rate equivalent Breadth of coverage Impact of activity use market research				
Main exhibition organize		Stand is favourable, commented on Budget figure negotiate nearer time	Observation				
Main exhibition PR		See PR for high visibility – above	Measure scc/display rate equivalent				

Activity	Objective / Criteria	Measurement			
Demonstrations (10 off)	Attendance to 80% capacity of demonstrations with at least 100 potential customers overall, all staff trained	Record visitor number by category; staff, customers, potential customers, press, consumers			
PR (agency) programme	Each element obtains coverage greater than cost × 4	Measure scc/display rate equivalent			
TV commercial produce	Within budget, to time	Observation Accountant's figures			
TV commercial show	Five-figure response rate in total from Web site and call centre Rated better than competitor's commercials	Measure call centre and Web site activity Market research before and after			
Interactive TV slots	Adjacent to sports major fixtures within budget	Observation Accountant's figures			
Web site produce	To time and cost within budget	Observation Accountant's figures			
Web site launch	A five-figure number of visitors within a month, excluding repeats	Measurement built into site			
Video produce	To time and cost within budget	Observation Accountant's figures			

Marketing activity	Person responsible	What is success? The key performance indicator and its metric	Measurement mechanism	Cost of activity and measure	Value for money achieved	Mechanism works?	Future use of activity/ mechanism
Video launch		Comment in the press greater than cost of launch Rated well by customers and consumers	Measure scc/display rate equivalent Market research afterwards (sample only)				
Extranet produce		To time and cost within budget	Observation Accountant's figures				
Marketing training		All staff trained	Training records – feedback to confirm				
Marketing staff appraisals		All staff work objectives set; finally all appraised	Personnel records – feedback to confirm				
Call centre		Perform to contract	Checks				
Fulfilment – outsourced		Perform to contract	Checks				
Telemarketing		Perform to contract	Checks				
Market research – outsourced		Perform to contract	Checks				
Market research – in-house		Attitudes/awareness found or trend recorded Satisfactory measurement when used as a mechanism	Produce answers – information for decision taking				

Outsource contracts	To time and cost within budget Meet the brief	Observation Accountant's figures			
New product development	Attitudes/awareness found or trend recorded	Produce answers – information for decision			
Re-launch product questionnaire	To same time as re-launch Ideal response to be at 200 per week Useful comments resulting	Observation Record response quantity and quality Comments found to be positively useful			
Corporate branding review (complete two months before main exhibition)	Satisfactory completion mid-year Allows rectification at main exhibition possibility	Receive report and recommendations by mid-year			
Brand policing	No transgressions reported	Observation			

1. Sell the existing range of products, with the new revamped basic product, to achieve the target sales (a figure in £s is included here) within the calendar year.
2. Grow the customer base by 10 per cent; that is 40 new long-term customers by the end of the year.
3. Establish the new media, with interactive TV and Web site operating in the next six months.
4. Achieve a profile at the end of the year that places the perception and image of this firm and its products above your direct competitor (list of attributes, benefits, features to be agreed by end January).
5. Take a stand at the main – category – sport exhibition.
6. Raise the awareness to 80 per cent by the end of the year among those that play, spectate or train in the sport, of the purpose of your business and the concept – products/services – it provides.

Illustrative marketing objectives and marketing activities
Table 3.1 on pages 34–39 gives illustrative marketing objectives and marketing activities based on the illustrative business objectives above.

For a full discussion on how to determine the most appropriate marketing communications for any situation, there is another Kogan Page book that covers the subject, *Strategic Marketing Communications* by P R Smith, Chris Berry and Alan Pulford. The book offers the SOSTAC process (Situation, Objectives, Strategy, Tactics, Action, Control), which should be adopted before developing options within the resource limitations, with senior management support and with everything in place before any activity is started.

Chapters 4 to 13 in this book cover the marketing activities – the 'T' for tactics of the SOSTAC mnemonic – just for direct marketing.

OPERATIONAL SUPPORT: DIRECT MARKETING 'MUST HAVES'

Customer relationship marketing (CRM)

CRM gives the right information so you can match your products, your media and channels in highly targeted campaigns to deliver unprecedented results. CRM allows a detailed analysis of customer buying patterns and behaviour so it is easy to create perfect cross-selling and up-selling opportunities. CRM retains customers by giving an understanding of their preferences, adding real value to the sale by making a bespoke offer based on predicted lifetime customer value. CRM allows you to profile your customers, with which knowledge it is easy to target more effectively. CRM captures data, cleans and enriches it by cross-referencing every source from within a business. This gives a leading edge on competitors.

Informatica, a CRM and e-business software and hardware supplier, offers business models. It has found that people are unsure what to do with information they collect for CRM purposes. People need help with knowledge management to decide outputs – who requires what information. CRM, once configured, can help with:

- contact management;
- sales;
- e-mail response management;
- supply chain management;
- inventory management;
- operational management;
- sales automation – e-sales in particular;
- customer service support – both for call centres and the Internet;
- marketing automation – feeding back marketing activity such as advertising, banner ads.

Experian uses Informatica to manage 780 million consumers in 18 countries with 1,500 product outputs available to clients regarding direct marketing (and consumer and business credit ratings). Borders uses Informatica to manage 700,000 book titles with over 10 million books, music and videos in stock.

E-Business has the ability to leverage data, integrates all sources, cleans and enriches, reads Web data, supports B2B, has near real time analysis and the outputs are scaleable. It allows targeted marketing. Advertising, catalogue, commerce, personalization, registration and transaction servers are supplied.

CRM has suffered from a bad press recently. Alan Mitchell writing in *Marketing Business* (November 2001) says the basic CRM theory is as robust as ever, but the problem is fourfold:

■ Not all the software is yet fully capable of giving a rounded view of each customer.
■ Consistency from the customer perspective through the use of CRM has not been achieved.
■ Assessing lifetime customer value in both financial and non-financial terms has still to be developed to a useful point.
■ Company culture has not changed into an acceptance of CRM other than from early financial expectation.

A central database

Originally, card index systems were the database. Even in the 1990s, City staff were still typing out letters and envelopes from cards held in the index every three months, often taking days to do this. There is plenty of software available now (ACT, Excel, Access, etc), which allows a firm to keep a central database and multi access. Each customer has centrally specified data and individual and historic data. The centrally specified data will probably contain information such as name, birthday, communication details, financial data. Individual information will be specific, such as frequency of contact, hours and days when best suited to contact. Historic information may include order history, payments, etc.

In a professional firm with clients, centralizing the database allows everyone access. It also allows everyone to see who is the key point of contact and with whom in organizations the responsibility for a contact is delegated. Who is to make contact is determined according to contact plans. For professional firms the history of individuals and moves to new firms can be tracked. Maintaining contact is particularly beneficial as individual customers move up in hierarchies and move to new companies. Keeping in touch with old contacts can result in new business with the new firm. This is particularly beneficial if the brand values have been established in early years and the contact is then tasked with finding a service supplier for the service you supply in their new firm. This is helpful for professional firms in a niche, when the client merges with a similar body and one of the professional support firms has to go (a current activity – in 2001 – with firms of solicitors). Maintaining relationships may just sway the balance in favour of the firm that is known to those at the top rather than to a firm that has not built relationships.

The knowledge management tool

Knowledge management can be used to provide timely key information or intelligence about a customer and the matched product/service to a salesperson. General application of knowledge management can be used, for example, for a taxi driver to pass on the knowledge of where (with timings) are all the concerts, football match crowds on any day. That knowledge could be shared with ambulance managers – allowing a plan at any time for optimal deployment of ambulances in a county.

Knowledge management can also be used to provide knowledge about a customer at the point of sale – to describe, say, the general pattern of purchases of that customer – and present the knowledge in a way readily understood by the salesperson just when they need it (when the customer is standing before them or on the telephone contemplating a purchase).

Financial service sales people can deliver relevance comfort statements. Say the prospect customer is discovered to be an accountant, which triggers the knowledge that thousands of other customers are also accountants. Such a fact can be introduced into advertising copy or when targeting specific potential customers from a list of accountants (ie financial directors). For business customers the influencers can also be entered into the database and the information they need, provided. Customers taking a car in for a service assume the garage knows all about their car. Service reception needs knowledge about the car belonging to the person on the other end of the telephone. Even a very basic programme can solve the problem – service reception keys in the first three letters of the surname and a frame appears describing the car, the last service/repair and when the MoT is due.

In your company you will need to decide the information required immediately to hand in sales or customer relations or telemarketing and if the software does not produce it in the format required, use IT to adapt the screen so that it does. Modern software will usually allow this so that different users can use the extracted information from a database (Microsoft Access for example) in different ways. Knowledge management is included in some CRM packages.

IN-HOUSE DIRECT MARKETING ACTIVITIES

Here are some near essentials:

■ *Call centre.* In-house or outsourced, a call centre is a group of people trained to answer customer queries and, when in an outbound telemarketing role, trained to sell or obtain sales opportunities. An interface with the customer is required. Whether you need a separate group to take the burden off everyone else in the firm is a decision dependent on who you are (the business you are in) and how knowledgeable you need to be to sell. See Chapter 12.

■ *Web site team.* In-house or outsourced, a Web site team responds to e-mails. This may be part-automated or a function handed over to sales if customers have been persuaded to send orders in to you via e-mail. Forty-six per cent of UK businesses fail to respond to e-mails sent to them by customers.

The following are direct marketing activities that you will need for appropriate situations:

■ *Direct mail team.* This will probably be an essential by the time the next edition of this book is produced. A team of persons dedicated to producing mailshots within the integrated marketing plan.

■ *Fulfilment team.* For direct mail or a call centre or a Web site or direct response activity (press or TV) where a response offers the dispatch of material to the customer. Used by most financial and banking businesses.

■ *Direct selling team.* For field marketing see Chapter 13. Exhibitions, merchandising, auditing and mystery shopping come into this category.

4

Direct mail

WHAT IS DIRECT MAIL?

Direct mail (DM) is a personally addressed 'written offering' that is creatively presented, usually sent via Royal Mail, with some form of response mechanism – not forgetting the envelope.

Direct mail is sent to existing customers from a database list created in-house or sent out using a generated list or a bought-in list for identified prospects. 'List' is a misnomer in that such lists are held electronically and usually supplied online or on CD ROM (usage and value determining the cost – usually expressed in £s per thousand per use). A list can be generated by another marketing activity (such as responses to an advertisement). Purchasing a list that has been generated by a list broker, may need to be carefully checked for the customer profile as its original purpose may not match your intended use. You must also have the individual customer's name correct – it can be a turn-off for a customer if their name is misspelt. The list must be accurate. Test it – ask for a sample, call or mail those listed to check accuracy.

In case you were wondering – some 4.6 billion items of direct mail were sent in 2000 in the UK, three-quarters of it to consumers, the rest to businesses. Germany sends more; in France, it is about the same as the UK. Unaddressed mail is covered in Chapter 9 on door-to-door delivery. Direct response advertising is covered in Chapter 6.

The advantages of direct mail

Direct mail is the subject of much market research, some of which is difficult to prove. Some say that 62 per cent is thrown away, while 22 per cent is read carefully, with 16 per cent glanced at. The Direct Mail Information Service (DMIS) gives figures of between 75 and 83 per cent opened, with 53 per cent opened and read by consumers. Business customers read less than half of mail received. Typical target response rates are between 6 and 10 per cent according to the DMIS. Experienced practitioners might halve these figures. (Plan on this, ie 3 per cent to 5 per cent, and you won't be disappointed.)

Response rates are tabled in the Appendix 2. A typical cost (August 2001) of the basic mailshot itself is 50 pence per recipient if you are sending out to say, 5,000, made up of postage (mailsort), printing the contents – a letter, an A5 brochure – and C5 envelope and the cost of putting it together, design, control (measuring) and managing the operation. See the Web site www.royalmail.com for the latest illustrative prices.

Will direct mail recoup its cost? You may have to wait for re-orders to recoup the costs. Steel yourself for some agonizing waits, but to succeed you only need to get sufficient additional long-term high value customers who will buy, buy and buy. But how many? Work out early how many that number has to be, so you are not surprised. An example is given later in this chapter.

Here is a quick back-of-envelope calculation for a direct mailing to bring in new customers. Say, if your long-term customer brings in a bottom line profit of £340 spread over a year, then you only need eight new long-term customers to cover the cost of £2,500 for a direct mail shot. With a 3 per cent response rate, you would have 150 enquiries. Say you convert 30 per cent over a period of that year – that gives you 45. How many customers become long term – say 20 per cent – which gives you nine. Just OK.

You hope your mailshot list is a reasonable one. You may also wish to work out a break-even figure if you need a result within the financial year April to March; if the customer purchasing is uniform over the year you would probably need twice the number of new customers – that is 16. To use the bottom line as a success measure might be unwise in that case. If your customers buy on a seasonal basis, buying 75 per cent in the run up to Christmas you would probably be OK. To prove that you have succeeded it may be better to profile your existing high value customers and then show that the new customer recruits match that profile, to give that early indication of success without having to rely on the figures. Then you can be praised even though you may be showing a loss on the direct mail activity in the short term. The second year will confirm and cement the success of the mailshot. Direct mail will then be deemed a success.

A Royal Mail survey of direct mail practitioners has found that they think that direct mail is ideally suited for:

■ keeping in touch with existing customers;
■ imparting information;
■ acquisition of new customers (using a bought-in list – see above);
■ selling products;
■ raising awareness of a brand;
■ data capture;
■ complementing online activity;
■ changing perceptions.

And the survey shows direct mail practitioners rate the following sectors as good at it: financial, charity, automotive and home shopping. (If you are looking for good examples to copy, try these sectors.) They also recognize the greatest problem is accurate targeting. Direct mail is certainly suited to products or services that:

■ require a degree of consideration of a complex proposition (financial services offers), or;
■ do not need to be sampled (for example, wine is not normally sampled prior to purchase), though a sample can be included in the mailing if it is appropriate, or;
■ do not need to be worn to determine fit (mail order rather than direct mail covers clothing sales where detailed measurements are entered into the order form – it is a specialist area).

Think carefully, proceed with caution; if you do not have a profile of your customer or a list that matches that profile, or if you do not believe your message is suited to direct mail, your belief may well be correct. You may be throwing away money and considerable effort with scant possibility of obtaining a return. The same applies to *ad hoc* lists – say past enquirers after a previous product – it is just not worth using an old list sometimes, by the time they have been updated and their customer profile researched/updated. Remember it does not look professional or competent to send out mail to long departed persons. Names collected *ad hoc* at exhibitions (business cards in a hat) should only be used for awareness mailshots. Exhibition names are useful when a completed questionnaire giving some form of profile and qualifying information accompanies them.

Direct mail and integrated marketing

Research by the Henley Centre for the Royal Mail, the findings of a Willott Kingston Smith survey and Helmsmen client experience, all show integrated marketing is much more persuasive. It also matches the way people buy. Customers are not persuaded by a single channel communication and because customers like to have reinforcement of the messages to hand, in some tangible form, direct mail should be included in all integrated marketing. A campaign for example may consist of some advertisements in an area to attract a response to provide names and addresses, followed by a direct mail shot in the same area and if you can afford it, followed by telemarketing with two follow-up mailings, say to those who do not respond initially. A Web site offer should also be followed by a direct mail registration.

Immediately it is apparent that the cost of all this marketing activity suggests it is best suited to concepts of high value. This approach works, for example, for buying cruises, for buying cases of better than average wine (ie more highly priced, offering a better margin) to people who are likely to drink wine regularly and are likely to have the appropriate income (and probably live in the upmarket area you have targeted).

When direct mail has a strategic role

Strategic uses are generally to inform customers or gather information to enable you to take a decision on a proposition. Market research on new products or service development comes into this category. Direct mail is less suited to strategic undertakings where you want to know the probable reaction of a new target market (where you have no customers) as direct mail requires you to have a list first. But do consider piggy back, where you 'borrow' someone else's established list to establish a strategic need (Chapter 8). With a piggy back list you can target those on the list with a mailshot, which will then provide the information to take the strategic decisions.

Examples of a strategic use

An example of strategic use is when an acquisition has occurred and you want to tell the stakeholders about the changes and what these will mean. The implications of new legislation are other examples, where the provision of information by professions such as solicitors and accountants is a tool in support of their brand, rather than a selling means.

Budget information is often presented in a brochure format, sometimes without an accompanying letter. This occurs for example when accountants send out details in a brochure or newsletter after the UK budget of tax changes. It wastes the opportunity to include some form of offer in a letter.

MAKING DIRECT MAIL WORK

Direct mail is a creative package, which consists of both tangible and non-tangible elements. The feel of the envelope and paper, the layout, method of address, format and messages, are all parts of the basic package. Any additional items to be included require consideration as well. The task of getting a mailshot together requires a degree of administrative organization. The timing of the delivery – when the customer will receive it is important:

■ The mailshot should arrive at a time most appropriate for consideration – at the start of the weekend for consumer products, early in the working week (but not Mondays, perhaps when traditionally many meetings take place) for business customers.

■ You work back from the selected date. Most people grossly underestimate the time it takes to get a mailshot out. You can almost think of a time and double it.
■ Remember that the creative and design parts can take a month in themselves.

The customer, it must be assumed nowadays, is direct mail literate and the package must be optimized to achieve its objective. Qualitative and quantitative research can help here. The database of customer information plays a key role in the personalization of each 'mail out'. In the early days, the only personalized part was the address label. Now the letter, including personalization of any part of the text not just the address, the envelope, the printed literature enclosed and the reply device for a response, can all be individually prepared if the database has the information.

The objective – the purpose of the direct mail marketing activity (or activities in a campaign) must be clear. Keep referring back to it. Examples are – 'to get a 5 per cent response rate with 2 per cent converted into sales'; 'to raise charitable donations exceeding £XX,000 in total'.

A useful way to see if any objective will work is to test it against the SMART criteria. The letters stand for: S = Specific, M = Measurable, A = Agreed, R = Reasonable, T = Timebound. What it means is that an objective should not be vague: 'specific' implies a figure; a target, with the 'timebound' giving a date when the objective should be achieved. 'Measurable' means just that. 'Agreed' means giving an objective that all those involved agree with which.

Once the decision is made to go for direct mail, decide who is responsible for decisions and planning procedures/logistics to get the mailshot created and who is to produce it under the creator's direction. In order to measure achievement, you need to allocate a budget and delegate responsibility to a single person overall. As direct marketing usually relies on an internal database – and if you are likely to do more mailshots, then it is best to set it up as an in-house operation. Integrated marketing more or less requires everyone to be aware of every marketing activity to make sure the customer view is one of seamless communication. So, go for an in-house operation. If it is a first-time situation then it may be better to use a freelance specialist to come in and advise you, to avoid making too many mistakes.

For in-house production it is possible to purchase appropriate equipment to save on the cost of the direct mail marketing activity. The advent of desk top publishing along with the price drop of some printing and camera equipment, means it is now possible to justify printing in-house small quantities (say less than 5,000 copies) of material cheaper and very much faster. This means that material can be updated or personalized every time. It means you can test out ideas in-house and with a small group of customers before giving the larger run to a printer. Double-sided A4 full colour laser printers with scanners are less than £2,000 (as at August 2001). Professional digital cameras are priced at under £1,000. The computer with a sufficiently large memory capacity and software is also around £1,000.

If you use a commercial digital printer subsequently, then the material for printing can be supplied through the Web or on disk (CD ROM) again saving time. It is worth paying a visit to a commercial digital printer just to see how compact (even with lacquering) a digital press is – no larger than a small broom cupboard. To contemplate the 10 terabyte memory that it has is mindboggling. As an example, the time to type in, produce and print an eight-side A4 newsletter in full colour with photographs can be within a day using a commercial digital printer.

Another possible saving, but using conventional litho printing, is to use a 'gang' machine, which prints personalized mailings from computer on to headed paper; prints addresses and any messages on to printed envelopes; folds and stuffs the mailing and any inserts into the envelope; seals the envelope and then franks the envelope with the appropriate postage. Preparing mail for mailsort is also a possibility. This sort of single pass 'gang' machine – the speed of the service set against its cost in terms of capital and maintenance – should be compared with your present method. For example, an organization that offers to print in-house and quotes two to three weeks to send out a mailing for 4,000 – because a lot of the process is carried out by hand – may well mean that customer relations are adversely affected. Volumes of mailings should also be considered as a factor. A typical 'gang' machine can produce 22,000 pages an hour – every hour of every day.

The planning stage

Note: this book looks at the mailshot process from both the directional and operational view – in reality, direction and operational management may be tasks undertaken by two people. The best way to proceed is as follows:

▓ *Responsibility.* Give the whole job to someone. Put them in charge of creativity and the logistics, tell them the objective – the purpose. Agree with them how success is to be judged and how it is to be measured (it is a good idea to let the person with the overall responsibility for the mailshot come forward with their own key performance indicator and its measurement – but of course you give the job of doing the measuring to someone else). Give them a budget, which includes the cost of measuring.

▓ *Creativity.* Describe the target audience (in a profile) and the message you want the customers to retain. Assemble the facts that support that message, the brand profile and any other marketing activities in hand. To ensure you are consistent across your marketing, define the responses both desired and any alternatives the customer might take as a result of receiving the mailshot and have to hand the legal requirements of direct mail (see next bullet). Timetable the operation working back from the preferred date for the customer receiving the mailshot.

▓ *Logistics.* Decide how the mailshot is to be put together. The team you need, the space and timings for the operation. Not only do you need to check with the Data Protection Registrar that you may use your list for the mailshot, but the Advertising Standards Authority for what you say and also the Royal Mail to ensure your package does not violate any postal regulations. (See the Appendix 3.)

Design stage

First, think customer. Customers are becoming increasingly direct mail literate and direct mail cynical. The material should of course be stimulating, interesting, relevant and readable. The objective – the purpose – needs to be kept in mind along with the profile, limits of perception and understanding of the customer. It is no good being too clever and winning a design award for creativity if it doesn't bring in sufficient customers. Actually direct marketers do not usually fall into this trap, it is usually advertisers, but... there are always a few.

Prepare rough layouts and copy and test alternatives – the initial package will no doubt be revised a number of times, and time should be allowed for this. The package will include some of the following, but you must have a letter – people expect it. The letter is what they read first:

■ *The letter.* This tells the story and gives the individual spin. It is easy to get carried away. It should be written in a personal way – including a touch of humanity, just as if you were there talking to them. The amount to include depends on where you are in the relationship with each individual customer. The letter should flow; sort this out by putting what you have to say as a series of bullet points and then work out how to link them into a story. Keep the attention going and strike a chord to draw them into the letter. For example 'why is it that in a queue in a bank you always have to wait'. Be clear and up front about what is expected of the customer – an order, a request for a trial pack, a completed questionnaire. Remember, the letter is the communication document – the eye hopes it will be easy and pleasing to read; the fingers will judge the quality, smoothness or roughness and weight, the nose will detect if there is any smell. Include three things – the benefits of what you are selling, the real advantage and make an offer. Also, pay attention to the following details:

  – *Header and footer.* Just include information that is relevant to that mailshot. It can include reinforcing messages or show cross-selling opportunities. For example, a builder could include reference to wiring, plastering skills when quoting for a roofing job. The header and footer should be neat and complement the layout. Your logo is probably here plus your memberships of trade or professional bodies. This is comfort information.

  – *Length.* The length of the letter should be whatever is appropriate. Avoid rambling. Do not necessarily cram everything on to one side of A4. If you have things to say that are selling then continue over the page, but break copy mid-sentence so they know it goes on to the next page.

- *Offer a welcoming greeting.* With a modern database you should be able to do better than 'Dear Sir or Madam'. The form of greeting should be as the customer prefers it. Generally under the age of 50 in the UK you are probably safe with a first name if that is appropriate. Over age 60 the recipient may prefer a title of Mr or Mrs. The greeting should be warmer and personalized. If you have no name it may be possible to give a clue in your welcome about the content – 'Dear Wine Connoisseur', 'Dear Parent'. In any case, the first sentence of the first paragraph should include a hint about what is to come. 'As someone with an appreciation of fine wines...' See more on this in the next two bullets. Test the welcome because it sets the attitude of the reader.
- *First sentence heading.* This is like a poster and sums up the essence of the mailshot. It should include a benefit. If possible, add drama. The award winning mailshot of First Direct was 'Why First Direct gives you more than you expect from a bank – including £15 right now, just for opening a current account'. An interesting fact or a challenging state-ment can provide drama. For example, the fact that direct marketing spend in the UK in 2001 is the largest part of marketing activity is fairly dramatic.
- *First paragraph.* The first paragraph says what you are selling – the up front bit. Judith Donovan says the golden rule is short words, short sentences, short paragraphs. Use two columns across the page for people used to newsprint. Only solicitors and accountants write across the page – if you don't believe it – try two columns alongside across the page and test it on customers.
- *Use sub-headings.* Split the message into readable chunks each with a sub-heading. They provide visual interest and allow a letter to be skim read.
- *Core proposition.* Indent this as a separate paragraph. This catches the eye and will be assumed to be important by the reader. Do not overuse this device.
- *Colour, underlining, using bold or italic text and font size.* These devices draw the eye. Be careful with colour – some colours do not show up well in some lights – and some people are colour blind. Do not overuse underlining or emboldening; it irritates the reader if nearly everything is being flagged up as

important. If the reader is over 50, use a font size of 12pt or larger. You may wish to offer 'small print' in a larger size in any case. Only use 'you', never 'we' or 'I'.

- *Use a PS*. A PS begs to be read. Do not repeat anything or use a meaningless platitude such as 'Have a Merry Christmas', but use it to sell and add something else. For example, 'remember interest free credit is available on all our sofas'. Even use a PPS as well.
- *Response*. Say what you want the customer to do: 'write a cheque and post it in the enclosed envelope with a completed order form', 'call a number with your credit card to hand', 'visit a Web site with your credit card to hand'. Tell the customer what other information they will be asked for.

■ *The envelope*. The opportunity to get a sales message across on the envelope should be taken. Each mailshot should be judged individually for the envelope sets the attitude of the customer even before the envelope is opened. People recognize bank or credit card printed envelopes with statements and approach them with not too much enthusiasm, but a bank letter for example does represent a large stable organization and does impress some people. It may be appropriate sometimes to have a plain envelope. Use a window envelope to save having to have individual printing.

In this day and age it is easy enough to print individually on both envelope and the letter. Royal Mail franking may obscure your message, so you may prefer to print your own – called Postage Paid Impression (PPI) for which you will need a licence. The benefit of PPI is that as part of the franking you can print a marketing message; this gives an indication of status to a letter for some people. Add a return-to-sender address; it enables you to update your database. Equally, if it is hand stamped or even better handwritten, how do you react? Consider them both for small mailshots. People do notice a heavyweight envelope, hand addressing and a real postage stamp. Here are some other points to consider:

- *Message on the envelope*. Use one. If a person of known calibre – a practitioner – within your sector, is named as an endorser on the quality envelope, your customer may be intrigued and interested in finding out more. Perhaps use the first line of your first sentence of your first paragraph of your letter, but end halfway through with dots... Do not lie: giving false privacy markings or 'important documents enclosed' are lies. People are wary of 'you have been selected as one of the few in SW45 for this special offer' as they may see the postman or woman passing them, clearly weighed down by hundreds of mailshots for 'the few'.

- *Size matters.* Size may be dictated by the contents – the brochure. It is more impressive if you use a larger envelope; you will need to weigh up the cost, but there are many stories about better response rates for larger envelopes.
- *Tear offs/reminders.* The flap of the envelope is sometimes printed to remind people what has to be enclosed (like VAT returns). The flap can be enlarged (known as a bangtail) with a tear off part to recommend a friend or entice customers with an extra offer at the last minute.

▪ *Reply device.* Print these individually with the customer name and address, making it easy for the customer to respond and easier for you to record the responses by preventing errors because of illegible handwriting. You will probably save on the time taken to decipher, for any extra cost involved. Include a 'trace code' so you can identify the mailshot when the response arrives. Even if you are also inviting calls to a call centre or giving a Web site address, a reply device gives a clear indication to the customer that you are expecting a response.

You need to think about whether a response card or the return of a form in an envelope is better. Requesting information responses is suited to a card. If you are expecting cheques for orders or orders giving credit card numbers or asking for information perceived as confidential – go for an envelope. The response card can be fairly simple, but use it to start a relationship by asking for information that enhances the database while including other tick boxes asking for further brochures, etc. Any envelopes or response cards will need to be thought through and printed – probably freepost and first class indicating importance and urgency.

The format of the response form to go in the envelope should make it easy for people to buy. Relate it, from experience, to typical order size. Listing all products with tick boxes, alongside order quantity and total cost (known as laundry lists) often persuades people to order more. Blank order forms, which are filled in by the customer, are less easy to complete but require a smaller form. To persuade people to order more, you could make offers such as 'free delivery on orders over £30' or make free offers if more than a certain value of order is reached.

▓ *Other material you may include* (which should be appropriate and relevant to the mailshot). Be wary of including too much in the mailshot in case it reduces the impact of your message. You may wish to include:

- *The brochure.* This is literature about the concept(s) – the product/service(s) – you are offering, included if the purpose of the mailshot is to sell. The brochure should be consistent with the letter – quality, format, colour, messages and contents.
- *A CD ROM or video.* These may be appropriate as an alternative to or alongside a brochure. The video should be no more than about five minutes but may be required to demonstrate a method that is difficult to explain. They can be very light nowadays and not add much weight or cost to the postage. A video is probably best used for consumer product demonstrations. A CD ROM can be used to give software a free trial for a limited period or provide a mix of photograph and video. Look at the CD ROM's recommended in this book.
- *Price list.* This is usually kept separate from the brochure to avoid reprinting the whole brochure each time prices change.
- *Incentives.* These are used to boost returns. Wine offers often have a £10 off voucher for a prompt response. A free gift – often photographed on the extra material – or air miles, are often offered with financial or credit card sign-ups. Scratch cards, free samples, free trial offers, free entry to a prize winning draw, etc are other examples.
- *Endorsement letters.* These are sometimes a compilation of satisfied customers or a letter from a personality or even a member of your firm – the MD or Marketing Director.
- *A novelty, gimmick, something 3-dimensional.* This makes everyone curious and keen to see what is inside. A wine bottle cork will do. Charities often supply a free pen.
- *Other companies' literature.* See Chapter 8 on piggy backs. Known as stuffers – they help defray the cost of a mailshot. This is you letting in hitch-hikers!

■ *Acceptance.* It is a wise idea not to take a decision at first sight of the final package – once seen, let it rest overnight before asking for a verdict. The final version needs to be costed and checked to see that it is within budget. Check the work has a clear benefit-biased focus, matches the brief and is set to achieve the objective – the purpose. Check the work from a customer view – pick up the sealed envelope as it might have landed (in a stack of other mail?), look at it, open it, take out the contents, read it – just as the customer will do. Think big picture, not minor details. Does the creative work match the concept – the product and service, the brand and is it distinctive? Does it add to the awareness, relevance, performance and advantage criteria or bonding, if it is at that stage of a campaign? The package should also be tested by a customer sample and their comments considered before final acceptance.

Production stage

Make a mock-up of the final package and test everything fits in. If you are using a machine then test all the items run through the machine, especially if you are machine enclosing. Ensure the database you are using is up to date and has been de-duplicated.

The artwork is produced as copy, illustrations, photography, cardboard engineering printing layouts, etc. This is relatively easy to alter nowadays with computers. Double check the proofs, including obtaining 'legal' clearance if required ensuring you are not contravening any codes of practice for direct mail. Check colour balance with a light box. Holding up a transparency to daylight is simply not very accurate. Insist on seeing any reproof.

Tips

1. To get past a gatekeeper – a PA or personal secretary is often given instructions to open all mail except hand addressed – you may find success for a small mailshot with handwritten addressed envelopes and letters, with a personal salutation and signature. (Even these can be digitized now.) Fixing real stamps on small mailshots may alter the attitude of the recipient favourably.
2. Envelopes with exclusive special offers should not be sent

out to areas with a large number of flats. With communal post deliveries to flats, it is often easy to see that many other people have received the same offer.

3. For an exclusive or special offer try to make it just that. Use a formal invitation on stiff white card to invite the customer to an event – a store with special late night opening in the run up to Christmas say – then treat the customers who come as VIPs. Liberty did this for readers of certain broadsheets for a time. Fortnum & Mason do it still – charging for the evening but giving an equivalent value in vouchers for the amount spent in store, with further discounts in store on the night. Jaguar are trying to change the image of their cars from 'as owned by directors of companies in their 50s' to the preferred car of the young executive (under 30s) as an alternative to the BMW or Mercedes. To achieve this change in perception the special offer – a VIP offer – is to bring to the showroom their own cars and then road test a Jaguar – an X-type – for the weekend. The customers would not have previously even considered a Jaguar.

4. Always put a telephone number for people to make contact particularly in business-to-business mailshots as sometimes your mailing will trigger an idea.

5. Use a tick box marked 'No thank you I am not interested', which helps update your database. Judith Donovan believes real 'Nos' do not bother, so those that tick the box may be interested later.

6. In many firms however it is often those at the interface with customers – sales force, customer service desk – who are the last to know and customers pick this up. Remember, consistency seen from the customer side raises sales as much as 30 per cent. (This is a researched statistic.) Don't forget, let everyone know within the company and any agency working with you (call centre) that the mailshot has been sent out, through internal marketing, explaining whom it has been sent to, the purpose and the expected response of customers. In practice, the campaign may often include a call centre that will be ready to respond to the direct marketing activity, having prepared for the resulting calls alongside the mailshot.

Associated topics

Lists/databases

A list is a compilation of customer information such as name, address (with postcode), telephone number, e-mail address, etc. A list in marketing terms is not much use unless it provides additional information about the customer – a profile – and you can use it to reach customers. The customer preferences, purchases, order history by product/service, frequency and value (so you know who are your best customers), are other marketing-useful bits of information. The information should be easy to alter and add to.

But a marketing list is primarily for use. It allows you to decide when to call, when to mailshot and about what. The list should allow you readily to contact customers. Computers do just that – holding a list on a computer, achieved using database software, which you can use for mailshots (see mail merge below), sending an e-mail or even calling a customer so saving a person the trouble of dialling. The database splits the information you hold on each customer into as many parts as you want (an IT person can achieve this for you). The separation allows you to sort the customers on the database by whatever information you hold. This allows contact to be tailored to each individual customer if you wish. Bespoke software that does all this is supplied for CRM purposes.

Information held for marketing purposes is quite different from that held by the financial side and though it is possible to keep both on the same database, marketing should be paramount – it is marketing that persuades the customer to buy – which funds the business.

You can build up an in-house database of customers, which is really a core asset. It should be checked as accurate and kept up to date. Names that have been collected *ad hoc* at exhibitions (business cards in a hat) should only be used for awareness mailshots. Exhibition names are useful but only when a completed questionnaire giving some form of profile and qualifying information accompanies them.

You can buy in a database – allow up to 10 days – you should check it for accuracy and how up to date it is. You should not pay for any inaccurate entries.

CACI Limited (see Reference Appendix 3) has over 20 years' experience of understanding and practically applying customer analyses by lifestyle, profile and location and for businesses, their type and size. The CACI ACORN system extends the ABC system into 54 types. Whereas the DMA Door-to-Door Council just lists households by postcode, CACI tells you who is there. The analysis is based on the census. CACI analyses can be used to plan door-to-door, field marketing outlet and distribution planning and locating. For example, some three per cent of the population lives in villages with wealthy commuters and 1.5 per cent of the UK population is characterized by high unemployment and lone parent council area dwellers.

Experian offers MOSAIC and also holds lists for direct marketing purposes of some 780 million consumers in 18 countries. DEMOGRAF is offered by Euro Direct Database Marketing. See Appendix 3.

Mail merge software

Standard software packages allow a process, called a 'mail merge', to take place between a word processor or desk top publishing programme and a database or spreadsheet package with the results sent to a printer for printing on to a letter, an envelope or label.

The latest software allows options matched to a customer's preference when a mailshot can be printed electronically by laser or sent more formally using a litho printer or e-mailed. The originator selects the output or allows the customer preference to prevail.

Mailsort

The Royal Mail has a range of discounts and services, which are available to users of direct mail. These services are changing and expanding, hence it is recommended that you contact the Post Office direct for the latest offers. See Appendix 3 for contact details.

Video, CD ROM, DVD

Using video in marketing is excellent for demonstrating how new concepts work, especially as they can now be used in not only the traditional video format – using very light video cassettes – but also on CD ROMs, DVDs and on a Web site. It is possible to 'film' in one session sufficient footage to provide a TV advertisement (at broadcast quality) and a video. Once material is stored – digitally – it can be readily transferred to other media. Display equipment such as large plasma screens mean that exhibition stands can also use video effectively and touchscreens in kiosks. Again, if you are new to video production it is wisest to use expertise. DVA produces a series of guides, which are most helpful. See Appendix 3.

The process of production requires writing a storyboard, scheduling, shooting, editing, graphics, animation, sound, music, duplication, packaging, etc. Clearly, project management is as important here as for direct mail.

Accountability: setting and measuring key performance indicators

If the objective for which this marketing activity is implemented is, say, to find new regular customers, those who will come back to buy again and again, you would probably want to measure long-term value, say over two years or as an alternative, measure the profile of those responding to confirm that their profile matches the existing customer profile. If you measure short-term value – straight orders taken against the cost of the direct mailing – then you may not find it a cost-effective marketing activity.

You should probably expect a return of a single low figure percentage for a direct mailing. The profit margin of the resulting single orders placed will probably not cover the cost of the direct mailing. But if your new customers are the same profile as your existing regular customers then you have a high probability that they will re-order. It is worth noting that if you fail to direct mail to sufficient numbers; you mis-target your mail shot or you did not test the copy, then this marketing activity will probably fail whatever measure you use.

The failure might stem from the original setting of the business objective and not ascertaining whether the objective is SMART. The marketing objective that followed should lead to buying a list that matched the existing profile of your customers, which assumes you knew that profile. If you did not know the profile, you should set that as a marketing activity before you purchase a list. You might measure that profiling success by taking a sample, checking their views through market research. You should also test the copy – that could be done alongside the market research. Is your offer understood is a key test question to ask.

An example of calculating the return on direct mail

Say you have 400 regular customers and you set as a business objective a growth target of 10 per cent, ie, you want another 40. Then, assuming you then apply the SMART criteria on the objective (see text above) and the marketing objective is to communicate an offer to a sufficient number of an appropriate target market so that they become customers. Then say, on a mailing of 10,000 at 50 pence per mail out, you get a three per cent response, then that will produce 300 enquiries. Cost per enquiry is £16.70. If the enquiries result in 50 sales then the cost per sale is £100. Depending on your margin for just 50 sales this is unlikely to cover the cost. But if the 50 re-order – that is buy again (and again!) – eventually the margin on their sales will cover the direct mail marketing activity.

The single measure of recording how many out of the 10,000 made a purchase is unsafe, in that you will certainly be open to accusations of straightforward bottom line failure. A better measure is to see if you have any new customers of your preferred type – your target market. You need to have already recorded, or put in hand marketing activity to record now, the characteristics/profiles of your regular customers including their purchasing behaviour. You now measure the characteristics/profiles of the new customers that made the 50 sales. If they are of a similar profile to your existing customers, then you could probably expect that you have achieved the aim. If all 50 match – well done. You would still find that you achieve your aim of at least 40 new customers even if 20 per cent are only single time purchasers. That would leave 40 new customers. You might, through additional marketing activity, cajole back some of those who made one purchase. If your measure of success is just sales and in one year, you will not record success. The better measure is a profile match.

Key performance indicator mechanisms

Measure cost per inquiry, cost per sale, numbers of new customers, characteristic/profile of existing regular customers and characteristic/profile of new customers. Confirm a match. Measure new customer sales, repeat sales, order values over a period of time for long-term justification. Measure cost of marketing activity versus target in the long term and the effect on profit. The cost of the mailshot is given in the paragraph on costs below.

What costs will be involved in direct mail?

It is wise to draw up a planning checklist. This should include:

▓ *data costs* – lists, data processing, de-duplication, checks for accuracy;
▓ *production costs* – artwork, print, lasering, enclosing, photography, incentives, postage out (mailsort), outer envelope, return envelope, response device, letter, papers (price lists, special offers), brochure;
▓ *response handling costs* – return postage (freepost), telephone (call centre – fixed costs), telephone (call centre – variable costs ie per call), response processing/fulfilment;
▓ *additional costs* – market research, measurement key performance indicator mechanism (measurement of profile?), supporting advertising.

Any information published in a book rapidly becomes out of date so it is helpful to have access to a source of costs that is kept up to date. The Royal Mail conveniently supplies up-to-the-minute examples of costs on its Web site at www.royalmail.com. DVA is also able to supply costs of duplication.

Code of practice and the law
The DMA Code of Practice is very helpful. It is available free – download it from www.dma.org.uk. It covers the use of data, offers and good practice relating to offers, information that should accompany an offer, fulfilment, quality of goods, gifts, premiums and awards, prepayments, post and packaging charges and redress by customers. Special rules relate to minors, credit offers, tobacco products and firearms, charities and free offers, network marketing and collectibles. Customer service is also covered, including complaints, rights of customers to withdraw, substitution of products and refunds. The Code includes references to the law as it applies to direct mail (and direct marketing).

5

E-mail and text messaging, the Internet and Web sites

WHAT ARE E-MAIL AND TEXT MESSAGING?

E-mail

An e-mail is an Internet-related communication. Access to the Internet with an e-mail address(es) is offered by an ISP (Internet Service Provider). An e-mail is sent electronically to a person as an e-mail addressee. It is possible to set up a mailing list of e-mail addresses. Software is readily available that will both address and personalize e-mails in bulk.

The complex technical processes behind the sending and receiving of e-mails are of no concern here. Of relevance is to know that individuals can exercise control – refusing some e-mails, diverting others to a junk mail folder. There is also 'netiquette', a mainly unwritten form of Internet etiquette, which precludes the sending of large numbers of unsolicited e-mails. Internet users may take revenge on those who abuse the system and send spam – rubbish messages – in bulk to those that do not comply.

Text messaging (the mobile Internet)

This is advertising through mobile phones. This media is in its infancy. It arises out of the amazing take up – particularly by 18–24-year-olds – of text messaging. All mobile phones can text message. There are some 40 million phones in the UK. WAP mobile phones in addition can achieve limited access to the Internet. Later technology will improve the capabilities. It is a global activity – over 25 billion messages a month and set to grow tenfold by 2003. In the UK alone, it is reported that in one month some 766 million messages were sent. It is addictive to those who use it. Some 50 per cent of 16–18-year-old boys now use SMS to ask girls out. A cult and language have developed with it. It is fast. It is trendy – this age group will not leave home without their mobile.

SMS combines mobility, intimacy, immediacy and the ability to push a simple powerful message to a receptive audience. There is nothing else like it. For marketing purposes SMS allows customer services, alerts, CRM, communication – a two-way direct response mechanism, brand bonding, event ticketing, the possibilities are still being explored. The first UK conference on SMS was held in September 2001.

People use text messaging because it is fun. Some 70 per cent use it for humour, 60 per cent use it to make social arrangements. It removes voice contact, which can give people greater confidence in communication. It is a wireless system and is not linked to a fixed line. The text is limited to 160 characters per screen. It is capable of displaying logos or cartoons on screen. Playing games is a feature. It is not a place to surf. Users can download ringing tones (10,000 are doing this each day). These ringing tones can be up to three minutes long. This is equivalent to a pop record. The quality of the accompanying sound and graphics is a future enhancement, which actually may allow actual pop records to be the ringing tone one day.

SMS advertising using the mobile Internet is in effect a permission-based lifestyle-centred communication, delivered via a device that is carried by the person and is often permanently on. A text message is short and usually pithy and uses the developed text language.

If your concept target market matches this age group and their activities, then you should consider the mobile Internet – there are excellent introductory (ie cheap) offers on now – as this book is being written (January 2002). See Appendix 3.

The advantages of e-mail and text messaging

E-mail

It is useful for keeping in touch with existing customers. You will need an e-mail database. If you have collected e-mails from existing customers then these can form a very useful database for marketing purposes.

E-mails can offer routine information, which customers like from their suppliers. You should make your e-mails of value to customers and worth viewing. To achieve this it is of benefit to include hidden offers – that is, make one-off offers within the e-mail itself or include invitations or other benefits. Then e-mails will be read.

Informing about new product launches should again be alongside an offer to make reading your e-mails an exciting purposeful process.

You may also set an alert and automatic e-mail response to potential customers registering at your site. The alert could prompt a salesperson to make a telephone call.

From 24 October 2001, when part of the Data Protection Act was enabled, it became a criminal activity to e-mail addresses to third parties without permission for the proposed activity. E-mail must be one-to-one.

Text messaging

The opportunities are still being explored but text messaging can be used as a billboard. It can be used as an alert – for example the mobile rings whenever a specified football team scores a goal or when tickets or a CD are put on sale. As a traffic driver, it can magnify take up of tickets and attendance at events. It is used for competitions to enhance branding. Here it is particularly beneficial as a two-way communicator – typically 40 per cent of users targeted from the customer database respond to competitions benefiting from a reward on completion – a branded product. Also, the communication allows the passing back of useful quantitative market research information to the operator.

AirMedia has clients such as Manchester United, MTV and Jennifer Lopez. AirMedia offers four products, which cover alerts, special news, behind scenes comment, and m-commerce (used for box office activity – for example Austrian Railways allow ticket booking through text messaging).

Example

An example of one list intermediary is Nightfly, a business set up by Diageo, the drinks company. By the time this book is in print, there will be some 100,000 under 30-year-olds who have signed up to Nightfly. Nightfly covers 11 cities in the UK with 30 channels with which the user can choose to connect. Channels cover nightlife – including clubs and bars, events listings, what's on on TV, hairdressing and beauty, magazines, travel, humour and fashion. Nightfly, with its Diageo link, is primarily an entertainment operator.

Diageo promotions of its Guinness and Smirnoff brands have included free drinks or two for the price of one at certain bars between certain times on certain nights on presentation of the text message on the mobile phone at the bar. These can in future be tied into a reader kept behind the bar. Many promoters however are content to allow much wider broadcasting of offers through viral activity and are happy with the extra trade generated. Nightfly has 10 fields for profile acquisition as part of the registration process and sophisticated monitoring of its customers.

Access to Nightfly channels is free to the user – the sponsor/advertiser pays the cost. Registration is through a call centre, on the Internet or face to face in participating bars themselves. Sony, EMI, some grocery multiples are now taking up the challenge of the mobile Internet with Nightfly.

E-mail and text messages as part of integrated marketing

A campaign can start with advertising, giving a Web site address, inviting customers to visit and enticing them with an offer (Oddbins for example made an offer to those registering on the Web site, of access to a previously closed section where customers could print a money-off voucher). Registering gives an e-mail address, a postal address and a customer profile to whatever extent the registration process extracts information. Attracting customers to buy then is possible through subsequent e-mails or direct mail mailshots. (Interestingly, Oddbins given in the example has not followed up the registration.)

If customers in the target market are using the Internet to order (and you can assist them to order over the Internet with incentives – even or rather especially business-to-business where the savings on administration can be passed back to a large extent to the customer), it is easy to extend this ordering activity to routine e-mail communication. If you are a trendy and youthful brand then it is almost a must for you to use text messaging as a part of your integrated marketing.

When e-mail and text messaging have a strategic role

Both e-mails and text messaging can survey a large database of customers quickly and cheaply. As in the previous chapter, for the strategic role of direct mail, strategic uses are generally to inform customers or to gather information to enable you to take a decision on a proposition. Market research on new product or service development comes into this category. It is particularly useful in volunteer member organizations for gathering information. There is a real benefit from e-mail and text messaging – you can rapidly determine the responses using software linked to survey responses e-mailed back to you (the same with text messaging). Snap Survey software makes the preparation of questionnaires and the analysis of responses via e-mail and the assessment of the validity of the findings very quick for Web users, with the answers automatically e-mailed back into the software.

MAKING E-MAILS AND TEXT MESSAGING WORK

E-mail

According to the Royal Mail/The Henley Centre, customers want e-mails to be addressed personally, accurately and to be appropriate in terms of response time and style. There should be standard response boxes, a telephone number option, and e-mails should be signed off with a telephone number and a job title. They should not to be used as a sales vehicle or to 'over deliver' on information.

To send bulk e-mails is not difficult using appropriate software (the Worldcast program for example). It is important to do this to avoid falling foul of the Data Protection Act whose provisions relating to the disclosure of third party e-mail addresses without their permission (using cc: for example) is against the law after 24 October 2001. The software, in a similar fashion to mail merge, allows personalization of each e-mail using fields and sends each e-mail separately. This does not take much time with the appropriate line (ISDN) and a high modem rate.

Text messaging

For text messaging, you require a telephone number list of an appropriate market segment of customers with all those listed giving approval for their numbers to be used. This approval for listing is often carried out online using Web sites. Equally, sales staff have been known to collect such information in a bar. A firm such as AirMedia can advise on listings and help prepare campaigns of text messages that match the customer acceptance of text messages. Such acceptance is researched for both frequency and acceptability of material. The user can limit the information she/he wishes to receive. At this stage of the media a specialist should be employed – with the opening offers the cost will in any case be relatively little. A contact for AirMedia is given in Appendix 3.

Tips

E-mails

1. These can be sent in a basic format or upgraded. Ask the customer their preferred format (browser-based or straight e-mail).
2. If you are to include exciting video or graphics clips and moving images you may need to provide links to appropriate software downloads.
3. It is possible to configure Outlook Express to send bulk e-mails but you need to know what you are doing.
4. It is wise to test each e-mail by sending it back to yourself to alternative e-mail addresses that you have, both sent as a straight e-mail and when it is browser-based.

Text messaging

1. Text messaging is still in its infancy and using a supplier is essential. See Appendix 3.

2. Beware text messaging spamming. A recent spate of spam text messaging has hit the USA and is not popular. This is because all mobile numbers are allocated to areas and easily discovered and used to call all users in an area.

Accountability: setting and measuring key performance indicators

E-mail

The purpose of your e-mail, should help decide what key performance indicators to set and what measurements to make for successful achievement.

▦ If the e-mail is a means to boost sales then you would need to know the present sales of existing customers and measure the result after sending out the e-mails.

▦ Remember that if an e-mail is directing to a Web site then it needs to sound interesting or offer an incentive.

▦ Initially most sites are found through search – that is people deliberately visit. Use an e-mail to direct them; they will be used to being directed to a site.

▦ Remember also that buyers buy through a buying process and you will have to attract them probably several times to the site before they buy. With appropriate measurement, you will discover how many times that is, before a purchase is made. You can use that knowledge when planning future campaigns.

▦ You may find that just using e-mail to keep customers informed about existing products and prices, achieves little – again this could be measured.

▦ Perhaps the use of an incentive would help – a sale or discount perhaps only to specified customers or the first 20 to respond. Measure the result. Again customers are busy people and may not respond to too frequent contact. Customers should be asked how often they prefer to be contacted – see Chapter 2.

If the purpose for which this e-mail marketing activity is implemented is awareness then some form of questionnaire – which could be Internet-based using a software product such as SNAP survey software (see Appendix 3) – would measure how successfully customers' knowledge is kept up to date.

Appropriate software is available for measuring activity on a Web site and tracking and recording how a person moves round the site page by page and the use of links. Repeat visits can be recorded. Discuss what you want to measure with the Web site supplier or the person who constructed the site. Insist on having measurements made of what you want to find out. See later in this chapter for more about Web sites.

Text messaging

The profile of a customer is typically of around 10 fields, with every text message out and every response in, recorded. Entry in competitions and completion of each stage is recorded. Take up of rewards is recorded – typically 50 per cent within the first month. Measurement and reporting can be tailored to a firm's needs.

Key performance indicator mechanisms

E-mail

Measure sales of existing products to regular customers and compare with previous period, measure sales of new products to existing customers. Measure any changes of sales after sending out any e-mail. Track purchase value and size of orders.

Measure cost of marketing activity versus target. The cost of sending out e-mail is small, especially if done in bulk. Measure the effect on profit. As a check on awareness, it might be worth e-mailing a questionnaire as a customer survey including questions to ascertain their knowledge of products and prices. Questionnaires can be constructed using the SNAP software and automated through the SNAP survey software. Questionnaires can be Internet-based.

Text messaging

This needs to be discussed with the providers who are effectively pioneering measurement systems. The principle should still apply – obtain measurement against your key performance indicator and metric – to ensure you have value for money marketing.

What costs will be involved in e-mail and text messaging?

E-mail

The costs of sending a batch of e-mails depend on the tariff applied by the telecommunication company and the Internet Service Provider, both of which can be very small. There are the costs of maintaining the e-mail database and the costs of the software to send e-mails. All in all, a relatively inexpensive exercise – ideal if your customers are happy with this form of communication.

Text messaging

The typical cost of a six-month trial using 5,000 users sending five messages a week is likely to be around £50,000. On this basis, text messaging is some three times cheaper per conversion compared with a mailshot or 15 times cheaper than a flyer or the Internet. However, as this book is written, there are plenty of offers now of £5,000 for 2,500 users for two months with design and other costs waived. Now is the time to test this market.

Code of practice and the law

The DMA Code of Practice covers the Use of Data within direct marketing. See Chapter 4. The 1998 Data Protection Act applies to passing on e-mail addresses to third parties. Permission is required to pass on an e-mail address.

A useful example of a privacy statement is given on the CIM Web site at http://www.cim.co.uk.

THE INTERNET/WEB SITES

The Internet is a global general public intercommunications network. For a business or organization, a Web site is an Internet site published publicly under an organization's own name. When a select audience only is allowed access through password protection it is called an Extranet. An Intranet is where the access is limited to employees only of the organization's Web site – such a site may be operated entirely internally.

There are estimated to be some 300 million users worldwide. Marketingnet, a leading UK company in Web site consultancy, describes Web sites as achieving one of three types of strategy for business use:

■ presentation – where people can look to gain information;
■ interaction – where people can communicate;
■ representation – where people can transact business (not just financial) without requiring personal intervention.

Marketingnet then looks at three ways to offer that marketing strategy:

■ generally available (Internet);
■ available in-house only (Intranet);
■ available to a select and targeted exclusive group of people (Extranet).

The way you follow the matrix of alternatives is your strategy – the resulting implementations are your marketing activities.

What makes a good Web site: effectiveness assessment

A recent report entitled *E-Strategy Insights* (summer 2001) by the Henley Centre and National Opinion Polls (NOP) for the Royal Mail has surveyed how to make Web sites effective. The report heralds the arrival of the second Internet age. It learns from the misperceptions and mistakes of the first age:

■ Eighty-five per cent of the top companies or organizations do not have an e-strategy, as at February 2001, though they recognize the future importance of the Internet. This importance is justified as over 50 per cent of the population of the UK will be online by Christmas 2001.
■ The poor take up by companies of an e-strategy in the light of that is a sad reflection of UK marketers. Annual UK Internet spend is £2.737 billion (£661 per person) as at March 2001, mainly buying CDs, books, holidays and computer software, yet companies do little to take up the opportunity.
■ Ease of use, convenience and quick delivery are the benefits to customers of using the Internet says the research. The downside is lengthy registration, time taken to load Web sites and perceived insecurity of online payments.

The report offers a way ahead, from a marketing view, for a company or organization as follows:

■ decide an e-strategy for the future;
■ integrate marketing activities with the Web site;
■ integrate the brand – it must be consistent in its online and offline forms;
■ match the way buyers buy – probably the most significant matter – often ignored in the initial phase of the Internet;
■ treat the customer as an individual person who is specifically seeking information when they go on the Internet;
■ influence or drive that person from offline activity first, to get them specifically to visit your site. Once on a site:
  – educate, when people go through a learning process to build up confidence then;
  – nurture the relationship as both a guide and enabler;
  – build up time spent by the customer on site and motivate them, offering a clear direct advantage and building trust in the brand.

The rewards are substantial. Once a site is a favourite, as much as 15 minutes per visit will be recorded. Many sites that fail to attract return visits by customers are unlikely ever to do business with them. The report says that attracting repeat visits will be the major challenge of the second Internet age. An example of good practice is *The Sun* newspaper Web site, which uses the same formula as the paper to retain customers as visitors. A failure to have Web-enabled customer service centres cost the first Internet age some £1 billion in 1999 the report estimates. That is, no one responded to requests for further information e-mailed by customers – mainly because no one was there, only sales order fulfilment. The total brand experience must be integrated from drive-to-Web advertising to fulfilment and personalized support.

Eighty-one per cent of all users go online with a specific purpose, and 52 per cent have decided on the site they are going to visit and the concept they want to buy before going online. That is, they 'search' the Net, not 'surf' the Net. However, 50 per cent of those who find out about concepts online go offline to buy them. What people want from Web sites is:

- ▓ simplicity/clarity;
- ▓ intuitive structure;
- ▓ low grade graphics (which do not take hours to download);
- ▓ up-to-date contents;
- ▓ FAQs (Frequently Asked Questions);
- ▓ contact us facility (including telephone numbers);
- ▓ integration with business and customer history;
- ▓ site and concept – product and service – should be recommended by magazines.

Informatica research findings are that a Web site must be:

- ▓ optimized for easy navigation;
- ▓ attractive to customers;
- ▓ intuitive to use;
- ▓ be quickly changeable;
- ▓ easy to find;
- ▓ responsive to change.

Informatica has client Web sites with 1.8 million visitors per day.

Strategic purpose of a Web site

Getting the strategic thinking correct is the business purpose of Marketingnet, which has produced textbooks on the subject that are recommended by the Chartered Institute of Marketing (CIM). The process applied is to define the business case, using research to assist if necessary – to find out customer needs from your Web site, then specify, design and after prototype testing, build your Web site. Subsequently promotion and maintenance of the Web site has to be considered.

The key difference of Marketingnet from other suppliers is its ability to produce the definition of the business case, which considers the purpose and objectives with a cost benefit analysis to ensure you get value for money. Technical considerations such as the platform to use, download speeds, etc are of importance but the ability to combine marketing messages and conduct business is too important to leave to IT alone. Sites that are not updated as customers require or are boring to visit, will lose customers. The Web sites must match the buying process and deliver the six Cs.

To update the site may require special training for staff on how to update. The site must allow customers to feel it relates to them and their needs. In summary, the site design and operation – as in all things marketing – should start with the customer. Like producing direct mail, there is a need to project manage production of a Web site to ensure the whole is produced to time and cost – which requires skill, knowledge and expertise. Also, like direct mail, the 'look and feel' must be right and, more importantly, the Web site must match your brand.

Understanding how customers approach the Internet should affect how a Web site is defined as a success and giving value for money to any company or organization. Clearly, collecting an e-mail address early, rather than requiring full registration (which is damaging – 42 per cent are put off by the requirement to register) at that stage and gradually building up information about the customer is a better proposal. Tracking a customer's visits and their length may also be an indicator of a Web site's success. E-mail should be used to respond to all visits by customers.

Many firms following a me-too policy, put their brochure on a Web site. That is unlikely to do much good. Peter Job, CEO of Reuters (December 2000), says 'Online companies specializing purely in content production are doomed'. The key to having successful Internet marketing communications is to 'think through the strategy'; that is ask how your Web site can help your customers. Think of the six Cs. That should help you decide the purpose of both why you are going on the Web and the context of your Web site – how it fits in with your other marketing activities as seen from the customer view.

The need to think through the purpose of a Web site applies whether you are operating as a business-to-consumer or business-to-business venture. This is the first reason why Web sites fail – no-one thought through the reason for the Web site. In a recent survey (February 2001), only a third of companies responded to an e-mail quickly, nearly half of all companies never responded at all. Tesco with £214 million orders in 2000 with 750,000 registered users and 60,000 shoppers each week looks at what its customers are using the site for and makes it as easy as possible for them to do it. Seventy per cent of items ordered are fresh, which is surprising. Tesco has 40,000 lines but find most customers buy only 400–500 in a year. Tesco lets the customer look at what they bought last time. Domino Pizza has a fast track repeat of last order.

The second greatest failure of Web sites to attract customers is the need to maintain and operate the site after development. As a yardstick, Paul Smith advocates a ratio of resource allocation of 1:2:5 for development:maintenance:operation. This is often the reverse of the ratio applied by inexperienced Web site operators. Setting the example, the BBC changes its Web site daily.

The third failure arises from a failure to integrate the Web site with other marketing activities. The advertisement tempts potential customers to visit a Web site. When they get there, they find the home page is quite unrelated to what they were expecting. The Internet site must be a part of a seamless, logical progression for the customer towards making a purchase. Fulfilment of the order is crucial. Many dot.com companies failed because product delivery was so poor. A number of specialists are appearing to assist delivery, for example, Addison Lee (which is also a courier), UPS, M-Box.co.uk (linked with Express Dairies) and I-force.co.uk.

The advantages of a Web site

Paul Smith when lecturing on Web sites offers five reasons for having a Web site and an e-mail capability. These are to:

■ help customers get to know you;
■ get closer to customers;
■ add value for customers;
■ build relationships with customers;
■ save costs (both your own and the customer's).

According to Paul Smith, research shows that customers spend more online once a relationship is established. Your Web site should change over a period of time as your business changes and your relationships build. You should plan for the changes when considering the purpose of the Web site itself. You may start with a simple site designed to attract and allow people to proceed to order/buy (research indicates that with the right advertising and some incentive, people will visit a Web site once). The site needs to include an incentive for people to return.

You should consider and then decide how to raise the relationship; whether you are going to offer improvements by offering greater exclusivity to customers through offers of Intranets and then Extranet membership or move from a simple presentation Web site to one where you offer the customer interaction, then finally allow the customer a say in the business (representation).

Just as for any other marketing activity, your reasoning for Internet activity should logically follow from your business objectives and the resulting marketing objectives. It should just be one of a range of marketing activities. You will be trying to reach a particular part of the market and hoping to achieve something. And of course you must measure it to see that you achieve what you set out to do. You may conclude that the strategy should change over a period of time. To accommodate this you might initially have a 'fun' Web site, offering benefits that you then extend to become an Intranet or Extranet. You may decide to be involved with a portal.

It is relatively easy to design, produce and have a basic Web site placed on the Internet through an Internet Service Provider (ISP). Slightly harder is to have the site registered with search engines and enter the right words (known as meta tags) that will ensure that your Web site is one that potential customers will find if they are just searching, ie customers not having received any advertising/promotional material from you. A lot of sites just happen because people are following competitors or have a fear of being left behind. For most businesses, the real problem usually is that they ought to carry out the process of thinking through the strategic purpose of the Web site. The Web site needs to be designed in such a way that customers will visit it and sufficiently often actually eventually to buy from you. This requires thinking from a position of knowledge. That requires a knowledge of both marketing and Web design. If you do not have both, then you would probably be wisest to use expertise the first time round. There are a number of companies that do provide the expertise. See Appendix 3.

The production of a Web site can be relatively cheap. Speed of downloading, easy movement between relevant screens, flashing icons are well understood, as are links to other sites, how to be recognized by search engines, the selection of appropriate meta tags. You do not need to be able to write HTML or XML to design a Web site. Avoid in any case basic Web-design packages – they are unlikely to be imaginative enough to make much impact. You do need to understand the limits of the technology – as with all media.

The difficult part of going on the Internet is producing a Web site that people want to revisit and here the 'techies' cannot help. You need to start with the customer:

■ What do you want them to visit your site for?
■ What will bring them to your site?
■ What will persuade them to stay on your site, persuade them to return and do that many times?
■ How can you build a relationship with the customer?
■ How can you persuade the customer to buy or place an order on line?

You need to have thought through the whole process – and from the customer viewpoint – think of the six Cs. This includes the delivery and fulfilment end. The reason a lot of dot.coms and the associated businesses have failed is that they did not think through how to use the Internet as a marketing activity to best effect. Paul Smith (1999) puts the figure as high as 97 per cent of all dot.coms that will fail in two years. He is being proved right.

The Internet can also provide a service as part of the overall concept. In businesses such as carriers delivering parcels and packets you can watch the progress of a package to its destination through the Internet. The service is part of the add-on benefit of having items sent by courier.

Accountability: setting and measuring key performance indicators for a Web site

This is where the 'techies' come in, but you need to tell them what to measure. Just measuring the number of hits is really useless as described earlier. Measuring unique visitors is better but does not mean the site is successful. Counting visitors who indicate how they found the site is a measure of the success of some other marketing activity, say an advertisement that leads them there. Where they have come from can indicate coverage of an advertisement. National newspapers promising regional coverage (and of inserts) can be checked by analysis of the postcode registrations of Web site visitors. You have set up the Web site as a marketing activity to achieve part of a marketing objective. Do not lose sight of this.

It is very easy to allow the 'techies' to measure everything by adopting clever ways of measuring and then you are left with masses of data, none of which may be directly relevant. A number of firms offer software that records where visitors have come from (which country even), which day they visited, which pages were looked at, where they lived, where they went on to. Clearly, a key record is 'who are repeat or regular visitors'. There is a need to communicate with those who register. What is the purpose of obtaining registrations if you do not subsequently communicate with them? You need to develop a follow up programme. Few seem to do so yet the research quoted by Paul Smith (1999) indicates that more purchases are made when a relationship has been established.

For example, say the marketing objective is to increase awareness of your products/services to a particular target market. Then you want to measure the number of hits people make on products/services and perhaps their prices on different pages. But visitors to the pages is not enough. You need to know if they are the right people. Are the people visiting your site your target market? You are trying to establish a dialogue – a relationship – so that you can find out if the visitors match your target profile. You want to establish as many facts as you need about them that define them to be your target market.

An easy way to find this out is to get them to register. You can then, by asking appropriate questions, find out if they do match. If you have not made the site interesting enough or they can perceive little of value to them, they may not bother to register. You may need to have additional information. A postcode can be identified with people of probable target markets. So you could ask for their postcode. People know that postcodes give an address – so they may assume that is the purpose of your question. However not all people are whom they seem – some use aliases, some use a number of Web sites, some will use deliberately misleading information. Beware.

You may have to offer an incentive that browsers may believe will be of value to them. An example of an incentive is to offer access to closed pages once they have registered – the closed pages being of some perceived value. SkyTV offers prizes for picking sports teams. Others offer games with a highest score to beat. Others offer competitions. You must fulfil the promise. An alternative is to offer a real redeemable incentive. By registering at the Oddbins Web site you could then enter a page and obtain a voucher that you can print. Presenting the voucher at an Oddbins store allows you to obtain 12.5 per cent off a case of wine. Some offer redeemable book vouchers.

Be aware that some site affiliations reward one advertiser through a roving 'cookie'. It just means that commissions are paid to links along the way for introductions and better still, purchases at the final site.

It is possible to complete detailed questionnaires and give permission to be sent e-mail offers of a particular interest (an example is www. lifeminders.com).

What costs will be involved in a Web site?

It is quite possible for simple awareness sites to be created using appropriate software for next to nothing. Firms abound that offer Web site development. Ask to see examples of a range of previous sites prepared by the supplier and ask for references. Take up references to see if previous clients are happy.

Charlie Dobres believes that no one should launch other than a test site at first. The maximum spenditure for a month should be £50,000 for a UK plc (£50,000 is no more than a single full page advertisement in a top newspaper as at January 2001). Test marketing – a marketing basic – should be continued as changes are made.

Interactive TV

See Chapter 6.

6

Direct response advertising (TV, magazines and radio) and inserts

WHAT IS DIRECT RESPONSE ADVERTISING?

Direct response advertising is:

- advertising in a magazine with a coupon or an insert or a tip on (a card glued on to the advertisement);
- advertising in a magazine, newspaper or print where 10 per cent of a display advertisement is a response device – a DMA definition (small print Web site addresses or telephone numbers are excluded from this category, though about 90 per cent of all advertising has a response mechanism);
- a TV advertisement giving a call centre number or a Web site address;
- a radio advertisement giving a call centre number or a Web site address;
- advertising on interactive (digital) TV when a pop up appears allowing you to bookmark/transfer to a Web site.

In a magazine or newspaper the direct response device may be a coupon as a part of the advertisement and usually has to be cut out of the magazine or newspaper. The tip on is a response card stuck on the advertisement. The use of tip ons is reputed to be much more effective than a coupon or an insert – because it is easy to use. Posting may be made more attractive by using a free post address. Giving a telephone number leads to a call centre – see Chapter 12. Giving a Web site address may lead to an e-mail – see Chapter 5.

The insert may be foldable and postable in its entirety or a part may be cut off and sent back. Some £536 million is estimated by the DMA to have been spent on inserts in 2000. This is based on an average cost of £25 per thousand spent on insertion and the same amount spent on print and production. The main users are financial, retail and travel businesses.

With direct response TV, the pre-runner to interactive TV (see below) the need is for clear telephone numbers or a Web site address as part of the advertisement and a large call centre operation to take calls during breaks. The use of a call centre is covered in Chapter 12. The Web site is covered in Chapter 5.

When viewers watch an interactive advertisement on Sky TV (a 'pop up' on the TV screen offers the option to interact), if they decide to go interactive, they press the appropriate colour button matching the pop up colour. See later in this chapter for a more detailed explanation. Research shows that on average people watch around 90 hours of a shopping channel (such as QVC) before making a purchase.

In radio advertising a telephone number or Web site address is read out during the advertisement. Supporting activities as for direct response TV are required.

Response to a direct response advertisement can be enhanced with the use of an incentive – it may just be a promotional video or CD ROM, which contains other material likely to be of interest to the potential customer. A gift of some kind may be offered if the coupon is returned. A request for a brochure is the basic response.

The advantages of direct response advertising

A direct response advertisement is best for complex products and services that require more literature to explain them, or where a demonstration or video or CD ROM is required. It is excellent for financial services where acceptance of the 'small print' is a precursor to purchase. It is probably unlikely to achieve more than that where it is not possible to give full details of the concept in the advertisement or the purchaser has to sign, accept and complete complex documentation.

Direct response allows a person, on impulse, to request to be sent more information or to make a purchase. This particularly applies to products not normally sampled or tested before purchase – such as wine. If it is more complex, it might be a request for a product sample in addition to the information. At least the respondent has given an indication of interest in the product/service in all cases.

The use of the tip on, with pre-paid postage, means people do not have to find an envelope, or copy an address, or find a stamp (assuming it is a pre-paid card).

Direct response as a part of integrated marketing

Direct response advertising will always require other marketing activities in support by definition. For TV, a call centre is probably the optimal marketing activity to use because a dialogue is established, whereas a Web site allows an opportunity for the so-minded to give scant feedback. For a mailed response the minimum activity is a fulfilment operation. Fulfilment means carrying out the agreed offer: this may be sending out the brochure offered and requested in the response. Fulfilment service houses will do this work. For call centres see Chapter 12. For Web sites see Chapter 5. For a fulfilment operation see later in this chapter.

Further marketing activities should be planned to take up the response or indeed lack of response. Follow up calls or mailings should be considered whether an order is placed or not, to try again to convert the expression of interest to a sales order, or to find out why no further action has been taken. To confirm that the respondents match your customer profile, as part of your assessment to see that you are getting value for money, you may need to send a questionnaire – the questionnaire could be covered in part on the coupon.

When direct response advertising has a strategic role

This is particularly when a particular channel is being assessed for a totally new concept for which presently no customers exist or when the appeal of a new concept to customers is uncertain. For example, ocean cruise marketers originally assumed that only the top CACI-type customer classifications would be interested in cruises, but found that they were of great interest to customers in many different categories. Initially it might have been wise to undertake some direct response advertising to see which classifications of customers would respond.

MAKING DIRECT RESPONSE ADVERTISING WORK

Direct response is an add-on to a straightforward advertising campaign. The procedure is as for any advertising campaign. The direct response mechanism should blend in well with the advertisement. In press advertising some tip ons replicate exactly the advertisement, but are overprinted, as it were, with the response mechanism.

Suppose the need for direct response has been agreed. This agreement should have arisen from a business objective that led to a marketing objective – probably to obtain new customers or increase general awareness. A series of options should have been considered and one selected: the preparation of a communication channel plan as part of that process. Out of this, you will also have agreed your customers' profile, though you may have more than one profile. So, assuming the decision to go for direct response has been made, it is now important to select the correct media.

Choose the right media

Choosing the right magazine or TV programme for direct response is crucial and you should use BRAD, NRS and TGI to achieve this. It may be wisest to select a broad range. You may at this point choose to use an agency to buy for you. The advantages and disadvantages are:

■ They have experience and contacts; they can obtain better spots and push others out.
■ They will achieve better rates than you can (but see the tips box in this chapter).

■ They need to be briefed fully – you need to be sure they really understand your brief.
■ There is a cost to using them.

In this day and age they should offer you an element of their fee dependent on their success for you.

Whether you use a media buyer or not for the magazines, radio or TV channels selected ask for the rate card, a media pack and data. The rate card is the offer, but through negotiation it is often possible to reduce the rate card figures. The media pack is to persuade you of how effective the medium is particularly over competitors. The data describes information needed in the liaison between your advertisement supplier and the channel publisher.

There are two parts where the agency or media buyer you use can be of great help for direct response. First, in negotiating all the matters of timing in whatever media used. In the press, it is more important to obtain a good position within the magazine or journal and on the page particularly good for direct response. A good position can improve response by 30 per cent, particularly for tip ons, says Judith Donovan. An agency can also advise on whether you may be able to get a cheaper deal by waiting later, but this may be at the expense of position.

It is possible to work directly with a channel or publisher. When you are working with a video producer, they can offer to directly supply your advertisement to a TV channel directly in a suitable format. Allow two extra weeks for the advertisement to be cleared by the ITC. If you do work directly with the press, perhaps it is sensible if you opt for an advertorial alongside a tip on or insert – that is where the editorial staff produce the copy and you produce, say, the inserts. Your printer can deliver the inserts to the publisher on time; packaged ready for insertion and your photographer can deliver your pictures in the format requested. A common digital format is gradually becoming accepted. All you need to do is have software that offers compatible outputs to the publisher's inputs. Your credit will be tested, unlike an agency, which will offer you their account facilities.

The way to produce the advertisement, copy and images is well covered in other books in the Kogan Page Marketing in Action series. See Appendix 3.

Tips

1. If you are wondering whether to use TV for your direct response, then remember that it is good for 'fame', quotes Michael Green, the Chairman of Carlton Communications plc. TV is what the majority of the UK watches by way of relaxation. If your concept needs fame, it can achieve fame rapidly through TV. Alongside the right programme with the right message developed for the target audience, your concept can achieve 'fame'. Fame is powerful. Fame is also fickle. Fame does not last long (remember famous for 15 minutes). If you use TV, it requires reinforcement: integrate TV with other activities in a campaign.

2. A sensible precaution if you are spending £500K a year – that is £10K per week on advertising – employ a media audit person to confirm the spend is as agreed and you are not being fiddled.

3. The media side will say it is impossible to measure anything. A person seeking value for money marketing would insist on it.

4. The creative side can produce advertisements that are so smooth that they do not work; a rough edge is better, remember. The advertisement should be within your customers' communication envelope – if it's too clever they won't understand it – test it first.

5. A poor agency can rip off clients, underpay staff and close the business quickly.

6. If an agency is screwed down too much it is likely to fiddle to increase its profitability.

7. When an agency is required to make major changes to copy by a client, for which it does not want to pay, leaning on the supplier may work and the agency spreads the cost over the next five invoices. It has not been unknown for an agency to seek out the printer and bribe them with whisky to stop a print run to allow changes to copy demanded by the client at the last moment.

8. The agency deals with the media owners and discounts can often be free air time/space. The client does not know what the percentage is in time or space and can often end up paying for air time/space, which cost the agency nothing.

9. An agency will often raise justified positioning disputes over the placing of material in print, say just over halfway rather than early right hand and the dispute is resolved with a pay back. An agency may do this as routine and not pass the dispute on to the client – or fails to pass on the pay back either (unless the client is aware and complains).

10. Certification can be fallible. Circulation figures can be falsely raised – for inserts where the charge is per 1000. Inserts may not be printed or dispersed as agreed. One example: only £7 million inserts were printed of an order for £10 million. Use independent activities to measure – use a call centre for example to verify by postcode that an insert's distribution is as agreed.

11. Posters have been known to appear on poor sites under railway arches rather than the sites the clients believed were being used.

12. Posters are carefully placed along the Chairperson's route to work.

13. Production can load a job plan.

14. An agency through incompetence may not challenge directors or photographers; unnecessary amounts of film may be shot.

15. Creative buying can be sloppy.

16. Challenging excesses every time is a basic start to finding out if you are being taken for a ride.

17. Cross-match supplier invoices – back up invoices and carry out spot checks, though this does not avoid dodgy invoices.

18. It is possible to find out if you are paying over the odds – being overcharged – for air time, by comparing network average against the station average. Similarly, an independent audit of production costs can be commissioned.

19. If your concept is to be sold through supermarkets you will be required to support your product with advertising assuming you want reasonable shelf space. The advertising will probably need to be placed in the in-house magazine. The least that will be demanded by a retailer is a marketing plan. Direct response may allow you to build up a mail order business with your customers should your concept fall out of favour with the supermarket and it is removed

> from the shelves. Ask customers to send in for a recipe leaflet – anything to get their names and addresses in case your concept is dropped.

Associated topic

Interactive TV

Interactive TV is a television with a communication facility. The TV set is coupled to a set top box with communication access through a telephone line.

To be able to operate interactive TV, the TV set must be digital. The BBC plans that within 10 to 15 years all transmissions will be digital – so many sets will need to be converted or discarded. At present (January 2001), there are 5.7 million digital TV households in the UK. Sky TV with 4.2 million has interactive TV on 12 of its channels (as at January 2001); NTL (about half a million) and ITVDigital (formerly On Digital) is coming on stream. BT is introducing ADSL (Homechoice in the Hammersmith area is a trial). Digital Sky TV users have free access to Open... which is the interactive channel (Open... is a commercial name). Though Open... is 'platform neutral' its ownership is 80 per cent Sky TV.

For Sky TV, to access and operate the interactivity merely requires handling the familiar remote control box, with a modification of four additional buttons. The button colour and placing is reproduced on screen and options to press are highlighted on screen. The set top box has two smart cards, which retain information such as favourite channels, credit card numbers, etc.

When viewers watch an interactive advertisement on Sky TV, a 'pop up' on the TV screen offers the option to interact and if they decide to go interactive they press a button matching the pop up colour to interact. They are then switched across to the Open... channel and a branded location. Here they follow instructions for more information or maybe make a request to be sent a brochure or progress to make a purchase. Open... describes soft use as using e-mail, obtaining more information or sending for the brochure. Hard use is when a purchase is made. About 10 per cent of Sky TV subscribers have made a purchase.

Interactive TV is set to become the greatest marketing communication activity ever, even greater than the Internet. The system has been operating and growing for a year in the UK. Already in the UK the Open... channel claims it is the third largest e-mail provider (December 2000). Twenty-five per cent of UK households now have digital TV (compared to 8 per cent in Europe) with PC and Digital TV penetration in the UK estimated as going to be about equal in 2003. Forrester Research forecasts that by 2005 more Europeans will be using interactive TV than going online to use the Internet.

Interactive TV has many advantages over the Internet. It is described as a 'lean back' media. It is accepted as part of the family. A television set is trusted in the home. It lives in the living room and is often surrounded by the family who all watch it together, whereas the computer is in another room, usually with only a single person in front of it. Interactive TV is put across as allowing people to go out from their homes to obtain information or purchase – it is not promoted as intrusive in any way.

Interactive TV uses telephone line access less than the Internet. The access is at the local or free call rate. Complex graphics and pictures are sent through the transmission signal. One disadvantage of interactive TV is that it is typically viewed at a distance of three metres away compared with a PC when viewing the Internet at half a metre's distance. This means that lettering and words and the effective written message area is much reduced – alternatively many screens have to be viewed. The logical process for a customer must be followed, if using many screens. There will be resistance to too many screens in any case.

The perceived and actual security is greater than the Internet. Security comes from the fact that the database holds details of the address and telephone number of the customer and the set top box has its own unique security code. The set top box is also installed – that is, connection is made to a specific telephone line – say by a Sky or NTL TV technician who confirms the address and telephone line number associated with the box. This means that it is not possible to steal and use a box elsewhere. The same applies to a credit card; using a wrong/stolen credit card causes a security alert when the check is made before purchase is sanctioned and the purchase can be rejected/police informed etc.

Actually using interactive TV, Open... offers a number of alternatives. Sky TV currently only allow the last advertisement in a commercial break to be interactive and it has to be 30 seconds long.

This means that it is expensive, though cheaper than an ITV advertisement, but note that Sky 1 is not far behind ITV. The price varies as to which Sky Channel is used. Open... is also offering shopping mall opportunities – similar to a concession in a department store – where a number of advertisers can combine to use one 30-second slot on Sky TV and then this is expanded on the Open Channel as viewers switch to interactive. The offer makes use of Open Xtra with fulfilment (delivery) as one delivery charge. It has been shown that many dot.com companies failed because they could not deliver – had not thought through the management of the whole operation. Open... is trying to overcome this – and maintain its reputation.

The technical support available from Open... to set up an interactive TV advertisement includes the use of templates, which conform to the preferred operation of the remote control and what is shown and where it is on screen. In effect, the screen size is less than on the Internet to make it user-friendly. There is scope to include a jump to a complete Web site equivalent (Open... does not advocate putting a standard Web page on the TV screen, preferring a cut down page for easier viewing).

What interactive TV can do

The commercial links between Sky TV and Open... now mean that the two databases can be combined. Sky TV knows who its subscribers are – from a profile drawn up at installation, though who is watching what still has to be obtained through audience research at any time. The databases will be capable of storing the channel and viewing preferences of the subscriber. The situation changes the moment the subscriber switches to Open.

The Open... database tracks interactivity and purchases. Clearly specific channel purchase will identify purchaser and buying interests from billing details. It will be possible to data mine, giving an ability to target at a later date. The smart card capacity in the set top box will allow some 100 loyalty cards. Open... will also allow shortly a 'store and forward' facility, enabling a customer to earmark an interest in a product without disturbing the watching of a programme. Interactive screens will also allow the product to be shown in colour variants. A 'jump to' facility will offer extras such as 'call me'; that is, giving permission to be telephoned. Transactions can take place while still watching once details of credit cards are entered on a smart card in the set top box. A 'call polling' facility, if enabled, will allow access to customer data. Retailers will be able to offer discounts online in real time.

The commercial situation, after one year (as at November 2000), is that interactive TV is being used to purchase in order of popularity: pizzas, mobile phones, CDs and DVDs. Woolworths find that even selling only 275 entertainment products (normally nearer 15,000 product lines are found in the average store) the interactive TV sales are equivalent to a store in 173rd place of their 800 outlets. Mobile phone sales are equal to two flagship stores in Oxford Street. A high street bank (HSBC) finds its interactive sales activity equivalent to 12 medium-sized banks. And people buy at all times not just during the day. One product launch promotion secured 3,000 orders in three hours between 4 am and 7 am.

TV producers have yet to consider how they could enhance their productions by adding in-depth programme material. This could include advertisements. In the near future, it will be possible to interact during programmes and offer people the choice of products including clothes being worn and used by actors; 'as seen on TV', showing products on a TV programme will be in real time. Playing TV game show games is another huge growth area presently under research; the potential for advertisers with universal game show participation is still being explored. Open... has trialed a Trivial Pursuit Game five times and obtained 1.6 million entries using a prime time telephone number, which has proved to be a substantial revenue generator.

A limitation to growth of interactive TV may be the use of TIVO sets, which have the storage capacity to allow purchasers of the TIVO set top box to remove advertisements. However, this is offset by the ability of viewers to purchase products through 'as seen on TV' promotions in parallel with programmes through the 'pop up' facility. The industry expects that a hard core of 5 per cent of subscribers will resist seeing advertisements on TV using TIVO.

Careful selection of the platform with which to go interactive is important. Open... is not actually an open channel. Each channel operates with different systems; there is no standard. This adds to cost if more than one platform is proposed, as the same material for interactive TV has to be reprocessed. It is not possible to create the material once and publish it everywhere. Each platform has quite different demographics. Middle England does now subscribe. The over-50 age group and the disabled make great use of interactive TV.

It is normally recommended for any TV advertisement that an alternative response mechanism is given, such as a Web site address or call centre telephone number or both.

Accountability: setting and measuring key performance indicators

A benefit is that direct response advertising allows the advertiser to see the effectiveness of the advertisement nearly instantaneously. You can tell from the response whether the target customer does match that claimed by the media. This accountability is not always favoured by advertising agencies. Force them to measure achievement on your terms.

A simple printed code can be used on the coupon and all returns recorded against that advertisement. Follow up by a call centre is covered under the call centre section in Chapter 12. A fulfilment house will record and collate all the coupon or questionnaire information, by date if you require it. See later below for further information on fulfilment operations.

Achievement may be a predetermined percentage response to the advertisement. Unless you are selling a once-per-lifetime purchase product about which no one is going to ask advice, the real achievement is how many become customers/influencers in the longer term. A tracking system will be required to follow the stages leading up to an order being placed. Initial orders placed may be insufficient to cover the cost of the marketing activities. The same key performance indicator measurement as in direct mail apply – see Chapter 4. The aim must be to build up long-term customers – which leads back nicely to the careful selection of the magazine or TV programme, which is the key to success. It also presumes you have a profile of your customers so you know whether you have acquired more of the right type.

Market research will indicate the magazine or programme that your target market reads or views, alongside which to place your advertisement. Market research will provide you with an idea of the language to use and how the message should be put across. Successful performance may be an increase in sales activity in the outlets to which the customer was directed. If you decide on interactive TV as a marketing activity, you need to be clear as to why you have selected it and this will point to what you need to measure. Interactive TV is probably at present most suited as a business-to-consumer marketing activity, because watching television in the office is probably unacceptable within the business culture presently.

As for all marketing communications, you need to check that your target market is or is likely to be soon a confirmed user of interactive TV and that you put across your message to match the customer need. And you then measure the achievement.

Key performance indicator mechanisms

Set a KPI as the achievement of more long-term customers. Research and agree the profile of a long-term customer. Obtain information that will give you the profile of the new customers found through direct response advertising. You should also set up interim tracking measurements if it is part of a campaign. This will show where customers drop out and in what proportion.

You will also be able to compare the profile of the customers you achieve with the advertiser and their stated viewer/reader profile. Measure the cost of the marketing activity versus target. Measure the effect on profit.

Fulfilment

Fulfilment means carrying out the agreed offer made in the direct response whatever that is: this may be sending out the brochure offered and requested in the response. There are fulfilment service houses that will do this work. Banks have a fulfilment section in-house. You will need to decide whether to carry out fulfilment in-house. This may be possible if you are using a call centre to supply you with contacts.

What costs will be involved in direct response advertising?

Use the rate cards provided but be prepared to go for a reduction. The rates are typically a guide. Even as a non-media buyer you should get 15 per cent off – plead first time use. You will have the following costs, which are associated with advertising and response:

■ *production costs* – artwork, print, photography, creative design; with TV/video – filming, studio use, edit suite use;
■ *response handling costs* – return postage (freepost), telephone (call centre – fixed costs), telephone (call centre – variable costs ie per call), response processing/fulfilment;
■ *additional costs* – market research, measurement key performance indicator mechanism (measurement of profile?).

Tips

1. Inserts – assume about 5 pence per insert.
2. There is presently a downturn in TV advertising revenue (October 2001) so deals should be favourable. Use a media buyer to negotiate rates.
3. For a concept sold through a supermarket. Typical rate for a full-page colour advertisement in 2000 was £13,000.

See also the first tips box in this chapter.

Code of practice and the law

In addition to the DMA Code of Practice – See Chapter 4, for the print – you will need to meet the Advertising Standards Authority (ASA) requirements. For TV – you will need Independent Television Commission (ITC) clearance. For further information on both see Appendix 3.

7

Catalogues

WHAT IS A CATALOGUE?

A catalogue of sometimes up to 800 pages is sent out by a firm or delivered by hand by local agents of the firm. A catalogue operation by definition is an alternative to a retail outlet chain. (Mail order is in addition to selling through retail outlets.)

A catalogue is not cheap to produce. Customers pick and choose products at leisure, ordering them through the agent or by post, telephone, fax or e-mail. The purpose of a catalogue is to sell. The largest part of consumer catalogues is taken by clothing ranges. The major players, to remain competitive, are offering exclusive product ranges (by specialist designers). Business catalogues also exist to sell industrial and safety products. Many firms now offer what may be called a catalogue, but what is really a brochure of their ranges of products, as a mail order alternative to visiting a shop or trade outlet. Typically, a mail order brochure contains a selection of items available in the shop or trade outlet.

Electronic catalogues are available on the Internet. An initial download of the basic catalogue is made. When customers open up the Web site then additional information and prices are added to the basic catalogue. Orders and payment are made electronically.

Catalogues are now produced electronically in CD ROM format as well as on the Internet. A number of firms offer help with Internet catalogue design or sharing catalogues – particularly pan-European marketing to retail outlets.

The advantages of a catalogue

It allows a customer to study products at their leisure. Well known brands sell well. In business, when an urgent need occurs for a particular part or product, it can be identified from a catalogue before the call is made and the part ordered and paid for and/or delivery arranged. Typically, an account is opened and held. For consumers the ordered items may well be centrally delivered to the agent who then delivers them to the consumer at their convenience. Catalogue selling to consumers is often accompanied by offers to encourage purchases and extend the range to friends and relatives of the consumer. Finance deals are sometimes used with extended credit to assist with more order placing. The key is to start a habit of buying from the catalogue with the customer, therefore the product and service must be excellent and special offers are needed to encourage early buying.

There is still perceived resistance to home shopping, principally relating to delivery. Delivery has to be made at times suited to the customer and within a customer-acceptable period of time from the placing of the order. The DMA's Home Shopping Council research confirms this. Other matters of concern to customers are the competitiveness of pricing, value for money, the range, quality, fashionability, stock level of goods offered, customer service and ease of return of goods. The failure to accommodate a lot of these was the cause of the failure of many dot.com companies according to recent newspaper articles.

A catalogue as a part of integrated marketing

A campaign may consist of some direct response advertisements in an area followed by a door-to-door in the same area or the use of a bought-in list (often based on the electoral roll) with direct mail activity and an incentive offer before any catalogues are sent out to those that respond. This is probably wise, for it saves on the expense of mailing out unwanted catalogues and also starts matching the buying process as well as building the relationship with the customer.

When a catalogue has a strategic role

A catalogue is itself a strategic alternative to setting up trading outlets in an area. This may be a decision taken because the area has low customer density (which is the reason catalogue sales started in the USA) where it is unlikely to attract sufficient customers to a point to buy. It may be because the customers are too busy to have time to visit (why business catalogues of standard office products work). It may be to meet the need to offer extended credit facilities (how catalogue trading started in the UK).

MAKING CATALOGUES WORK

Judith Donovan believes it is easy to get the format of a catalogue wrong. Experience indicates the importance of how to set out a catalogue to optimize sales. Research has shown how the eye of the customer moves round a page and how a customer moves through the catalogue with the right mix of photographs, product copy and selling copy. Catalogue design is a specialist task. As when visiting a store, customers get used to a layout and follow a specific route through a catalogue.

If you are already in the catalogue business then you probably have more 'how to' expertise than this book offers. If you intend to start a catalogue-based business, that is, one where your sole means of contact with the customer is through a catalogue, then the best route is to use the services of a specialist. This is a direct marketing activity that it is not recommended without such help.

DIY, suppliers, agencies
This is not a task for anyone but a specialist. Employ a firm that has produced and printed catalogues before and insist on seeing examples of its work before engaging it. Ask its clients how well it performs. See also Chapter 4 for information on lists/database and mail merge.

Tips

1. Do not re-invent the wheel; use the expertise of others. See how the major catalogue firms lay out pages with photographs, codes and pricing of the items; see how a customer is taken through the process of ordering and the

layout of the order form; see how the catalogue is sectioned, introduced, indexed and where the guarantee is placed.
2. Break up a catalogue with special features or special offers. Right-hand pages are scanned by the eyes first – a device will need to draw people across to the left-hand page. Clear photographs are essential. Copy needs to sell.
3. A number of firms offer a gift incentive to the buyer for separate delivery to an address of the buyer's own choosing (when placing orders for particular items or of a particular value or by a deadline). This is a business catalogue device that keeps the buyers sweet.
4. Appropriate settings of the products in use will assist an understanding of what a product is for and suggest how it might be used/worn or placed. Assume customers have little imagination. It may well be worth asking for suggestions as to uses for appropriate concepts and publishing the results (all part of building customer relationships).

Accountability: setting and measuring key performance indicators and key performance indicator mechanisms

As a 'how to' book our focus then moves to how to select, measure and evaluate the performance of the specialist or specialist company you select to produce your catalogue. When selecting a specialist to help with establishing your catalogue, you should be given clear evidence of their success with other catalogues for other clients. Test that evidence. Speak to customers. You should set agreed measures of success. You should then monitor that achievement.

The bottom line is clearly the number of sales orders placed or credit sales and the interest generated as an income stream. Setting a target of the number of new customers the marketing activity is expected to garner is probably the best challenge. This should be based on the number of potential targets in the area to be targeted.

However, as implied in the previous paragraph, there is a need to analyse the placing of products in the catalogue and the pattern of purchasing that result from changes in layout as well as the actual sales. Again, this is the province of the specialist.

The process to achieve such customers may take time and when set against actual cost of the marketing activities, in the short term may show a loss. The use of agents operating on a commission-only basis may offset this by removing some or most of the costs of distribution and administration. Actual orders value should be measured and set against the cost of the catalogue and administration.

What costs will be involved in producing a catalogue?

The eventual achievement is of regular and valuable customers. Measure actual increase and percentage increase in numbers of customers. Record over time whether new customers achieve regular and valuable customer status. Measure cost of marketing activity versus target. Measure the effect on profit. Catalogues are expensive to produce. The quality of the catalogue and its layout will to an extent set the buying feeling of the buyer as favourable or not. It is impossible here to give a pragmatic quote.

Code of practice

The DMA Code of Practice is very helpful. It is available free – download it from www.dma.org.uk.

The Code covers the offers and good practice relating to offers, information that should accompany an offer, fulfilment, quality of goods, gifts, premiums and awards, prepayments, post and packaging charges and redress by customers.

Special rules relate to minors, credit offers, free offers and collectibles. Customer service is also covered, including complaints, rights of customers to withdraw, substitution of products and refunds. The Code includes references to the law as it applies to catalogues (and direct marketing).

Associated topics

Lists/databases, mail merge – see Chapter 4.

8

Piggy back mailing

WHAT IS PIGGY BACK MAILING?

It is just what it says: an item of literature included 'piggy back' with some other firm's mailing. For example, with a local authority letter or a gas, water, electricity or telephone bill or a credit card company (holidays, etc!). A good firm to pick is one that is regularly sending out mail to customers – catalogue or mail order firms are usually receptive. There is a belief that firms in the South are less helpful than ones in the Midlands and the North. The mailing would include or be itself a voucher or reply card to place an order or request for a brochure. The term piggy back is not always used. The terms 'third party mailings' or 'product dispatch' are also used. Take care in selecting your piggy back service provider. For a one-off purchase of say an electric power shower unit (sent out with an electricity bill!), where repeat purchases are unlikely, placing an order is sufficient – and to save time this can be done directly with an installer.

For a service or where repeat purchases are required – selling water filters for example by sending out a piggy back with a water bill – then it is worth pursuing those that respond initially but subsequently decline, so a brochure offer to obtain names and addresses rather than seeking sales orders may be preferable. You can add 'advantage' by providing an incentive such as a cost reduction to the unit, or free installation or with a cost reduction installation.

Servicing offers are another example – annual servicing and maintenance of your gas boiler – the offer sent out piggy back with a gas bill, but you need a name and address and an indication of the make of the boiler. Those that do take up the offer can then be sent reminders just before the anniversary each year. Piggy back can deliver a message to a particular utility user – specifically targeting a customer – in this way.

The advantages of piggy back mailing

It is probably a cheaper alternative than a direct mailing – you share the cost of postage and use someone else's list. A piggy back can add value to the mailshot it accompanies and is thus mutually beneficial. This is probably why utilities are much more discerning now in deciding with whom they will 'piggy back', seeking clear beneficial value from an association with you – you will need to sell them the benefits. Piggy back is often successful because of the greater precision of targeting and the carrier's brand provides a status and quality provenance not available to a firm – particularly one just starting.

Piggy back is more precisely targeted than door-to-door or direct mailing to a list. A gas maintenance and service provider clearly would waste a mailing to a non-gas user; a piggy back offer to a BT user is better than a general mail out, but when a BT-associated offer is sent out on a general mailing, it is not much help to a customer solely using an NTL cable line (as happens now!).

Piggy back as a part of integrated marketing

A campaign for an electric shower, say, may consist of local newspaper advertisements through local firms of appliance suppliers and fitters and two consecutive quarters piggy backs with an electricity supplier in the same area, followed by telemarketing follow up for those that made telephone rather than response card replies. Remember how customers buy and try to match the campaign to that buying process.

When piggy back has a strategic role

Piggy back can be a useful determinant of initial response to a new product or service. When you are a start-up firm without customers, then find someone who already has an extensive list in your local area and you will soon pick up business using piggy back if you have selected the right partner. The difficulty is persuading an established firm to offer an unproven business the piggy back opportunity – use your charm; they can but say no. More likely they will say 'Oh, no one has asked us before'.

MAKING PIGGY BACK MAILING WORK

Determine any service or supply organizations that are likely to have a similar target market to your own. Look for firms who are likely to mutually benefit from an association with your products or service. Call the firm – try their marketing department – they may not recognize 'piggy back' – so try 'affinity marketing'.

Negotiation will initially be about whether the product you are offering matches their business. Some utilities are very commercially minded and insist on a partnership deal. Contact is usually through an Affinity Marketing Manager. Once these hurdles of the match of products and service are overcome, discussion will usually be about the extra insertion cost and mail charging if it raises the cost of postage. An example of piggy back activity is Rowenta kettles in a partnership deal with Thames Water.

The piggy back should contain a direct response mechanism – the return of a coupon, a telephone number to call, a Web site to visit. You need to build up a database in case your relationship with your piggy back service provider fails. To that end, you will need to set up fulfilment or a call centre or have a Web site operation ready to pick up e-mails. If the response is to a telephone number or a Web site then those taking the calls or operating the Web responses should be trained on what data to collect and how to respond. See Chapter 5 for Web site activity and Chapter 12 for call centres.

The actual production of the piggy back material is similar to producing an insert – a direct response mechanism(see Chapter 6). As with all inserts, you have a few seconds to make your impact before your item ends up in the bin. The few words seen by the customer need to be sufficiently compelling for them to give a further look to absorb the whole message. It should be easy for them to respond.

Your staff should be trained to expect the response and know how to handle it. It is the start of customer relations with a potential customer – the opportunity should not be thrown away. It is important that your staff are complimentary about your piggy back service provider and they should be able to give helpful advice and a contact for further information should customers ask about the piggy back service provider's concept. Record such requests for advice and feed them back to the piggy back service provider as a benefit of your relationship with them.

DIY, suppliers, agencies

This is usually something you will need to organize yourself. There is no harm in asking an agency whether they have any clients who might be receptive to the idea of allowing you to piggy back with them.

Tips

1. You need to sell the idea to the person responsible for piggy back acceptance. It is worth having carried out a small amount of research with their customers to see that the match is acceptable – then quote that research in your discussions.
2. Keep your piggy back small; it should not dominate the package or the main item in any way. A6 is a recommended size.
3. Do remember, not everyone is pleased to see a bill. Think carefully about whether sending your piggy back out with a bill is beneficial. Why not offer to pay the first 10 bills on orders received?
4. Do not expect to send your gardening catalogue invitation with another firm sending out gardening catalogues. A plant/plant products supplier offering 'all you need to grow herbs' might well go out with a cookery book club.

Accountability: setting and measuring key performance indicators

Achievement may be a predetermined percentage response to the piggy back, though this is probably only relevant when a brochure is requested as an interim measurement of the success of the message.

The value of orders placed is of greater interest when you are carrying out a single piggy back with no follow up – which you would no doubt hope would bring in more profit than the cost of any piggy back marketing activity.

You may feel a benefit in sampling a few recipients to see if the piggy back was well- or poorly timed, or whether any incentive raised the customer interest. An offer to install gas central heating free may be well received in high rise flats where the cost of external making-good requires scaffolding.

A fulfilment house will record and collate all the coupon or questionnaire information, by date if you require it. You can set up a similar operation in-house. This is where you can measure the response in terms of value of data collected as well as order value.

If you are carrying out more than one piggy back mailing, use a unique code on the particular response voucher to be quoted by the customer when calling or picked up by the fulfilment service to find out which particular piggy back was more or less successful than any other. This may determine during which month it is best to send out piggy back mailings – is the poorest response in bleak January or in fact do New Year's resolutions hold sway say for a gas boiler maintenance contract? Test rather than assume when the best time of year is to send.

Key performance indicator mechanisms

Use a unique code on the particular response voucher to be quoted by the customer when calling or picked up by the fulfilment service. Measure the cost of marketing activity versus target. Measure the effect on profit. If a piggy back is less successful than expected check on the date (month) sent out.

Measure the response at the point of fulfilment of a sales order or brochure request in terms of numbers and value of any sales orders placed. Collect names and addresses for a database.

Measure subsequent marketing activity responses. Measure repeat purchases of products or services – this establishes real success.

What costs will be involved in piggy back mailing?

Probably the cheapest form of direct marketing if you can come to a delivery cost sharing agreement. See page 95 for costs breakdown.

Code of practice

The DMA Code of Practice is very helpful. It is available free – download it from www.dma.org.uk. The code covers the use of data – you need to check that the firm's data allows your piggy back offer to be included.

The Code covers offers and good practice relating to offers, information that should accompany an offer, fulfilment, quality of goods, gifts, premiums and awards, prepayments, post and packaging charges and redress by customers. Special rules relate to minors, credit offers and free offers. Customer service is also covered including complaints, rights of customers to withdraw, substitution of products and refunds.

Associated topics

Web sites – see Chapter 5.
Inserts – see Chapter 6.
Call centres – see Chapter 12.
Fulfilment – see Chapter 6.

9

Door-to-door delivery

WHAT IS DOOR-TO-DOOR DELIVERY?

It is non-personalized, non-individual, un-addressed literature that is hand-delivered via the letterbox. Typical examples of door-to-door delivery are leaflets, coupons, samples.

Delivery by hand is either through the Royal Mail (some 20–25 per cent) alongside the normal post or through a number of organizations that do door-to-door delivery, such as a member of the DMA Door-to Door Council (formerly the Association of Household Distributors [AHD]) (see Reference Appendix 3). Local newspapers also deliver door-to-door as well (about a quarter of all door-to-door advertising is delivered with the local newspaper according to the HBH Partnership).

The advantages of door-to-door delivery

It can be the cheapest method of delivering your message or sales promotion offer (other than piggy back where delivery costs are shared).

Responses are estimated to be up to 12 per cent compared to the 1–2 per cent typical of magazine direct response. Thirty per cent of customers surveyed by the HBH partnership have at one time or another responded to door-to-door. The message can be as complex or as long as you like. (It is very useful for a message that you wish every household in the UK to see, hence its use by government – the Aids campaign used it.) Door-to-door drops totalled somewhere between 5 and 8 billion leaflets in 1999 – about a quarter of all material pushed through the letterbox – according to the Royal Mail and the DMA Door-to-Door Council.

Door-to-door delivery gives blanket cover of an area. It does not discriminate. It does not duplicate. For any area, the reach/cover can be a very cost-effective method of direct communication. Typical cost of print and delivery is estimated at £80 per thousand. It does not require the expense of list purchase. It is possible to target quite closely by the profile of people living in the streets. It is also possible to set up and complete a door-to-door operation relatively fast.

It can be used in appropriate areas for local services ranging from such services as those of an estate agent (typically a free valuation) or a solicitor (free short initial consultation) or a haircut. It may invite people to try a service. Restaurants and takeaways top the list, followed by charities and magazines/newspapers themselves, according to the HBH Partnership. It certainly is a proven method of increasing local in-store traffic.

It is a way of delivering product samples with a money-off voucher for a follow up purchase. Samples of new products are often personal hygiene-related (shampoos, cosmetics, perfumes) with coupons for money off a further purchase redeemable at a local shop. Door-to-door is useful for a pilot or test of a new product launch. It practically introduces potential customers to the product. It is seen favourably by many, particularly when providing a free gift.

A door-to-door might seek a response, which gives an opportunity to acquire a name and address from those who take up the offer made. The voucher or coupon might ask for a name and address at minimum. The door-to-door activity may well be just one of a number of integrated marketing activities planned; with follow up marketing activities using the names and addresses acquired from respondents to the door-to-door activity.

Your staff should be trained to expect the response and know how to handle it. It is the start of customer relations with a potential long-term customer – the opportunity should not be thrown away:

▓ How often do you use a coupon and write or give your name and address for a meal/takeaway offer or meal delivery. Then you never hear anything again?

▦ If there had been a follow up, a bond might have formed.
▦ Regular customers might be rewarded by further vouchers.

If the response is to a telephone number or a Web site then those taking the calls or operating the Web responses should be trained on what data to collect and how to respond.

Door-to-door delivery as a part of integrated marketing

It is easy to add the design and timing of a leaflet drop to match a TV or poster advertising campaign, perhaps using the leaflet to explain in detail what it is not possible to put into the advertisement.

A door-to-door marketing activity can be the first activity in a campaign to launch any concept – product or service. This then produces the names and addresses for subsequent mailings.

When door-to-door delivery has a strategic role

When no list exists of customers in an area, it can be the means of obtaining a list of potential customers. It is a guaranteed mass market means of reaching every household. Government and charities increasingly appreciate this. It can be a cheap way to test the potential response to a new concept.

MAKING DOOR-TO-DOOR DELIVERY WORK

The objective – the purpose of the door-to-door marketing activity – needs to be decided first. Assuming a decision has been made as to the purpose of the door-to-door drop (which should be referred back to from time to time), the best way to proceed is to consider the following seven issues:

▦ What is to be delivered?
▦ How does it survive; long enough to be read?
▦ To whom is it to be delivered?
▦ How will it be delivered?
▦ What checks need to be made to validate delivery?
▦ How much will it cost?
▦ What needs to be measured to know that the purpose has been achieved?

What is to be delivered?

Clearly, a blinding flash of the obvious, it needs to fit through the letterbox and not be too heavy. If it is too large or too heavy then you probably need to put in a further stage to save the cost of unnecessary delivery, only sending out the large/heavy package separately to those expressing an interest:

■ If it is just a piece of printed paper, then be aware again of quality and feel.
■ How will it get though the letterbox?
■ Will it scrumple up rather than look pristine?
■ It may look best inside an envelope – giving the feel that it is a letter, not junk mail.

Remember, a lot of door-to-door advertising is delivered so your item needs to look and feel different. If you are putting together a package then it should be given the same consideration as a piece of direct mail (see Chapter 4).

How does it survive; long enough to be read?

It needs instant impact – the creativity of the material should ensure that it is visibly arresting. If it is enclosed in an envelope it will be treated more as a letter (see the tip later on, about envelopes). If it is just a printed piece of paper, it is an advertisement in effect, with a short time span. It needs to have a brief clear message – just in case it is thrown into the bin at once.

A clear offer such as 'free delivery' may be sufficient. This begs the question of the recipient – what is coming that has 'free delivery'? It must have value in the eyes of the recipient. If every pizza delivery is free then it will have no value. It does of course have to match your other material and marketing activities and your brand as one integrated part of it.

Try a different shape – cut outs may make an impact. You need to build up slowly to any complex message – which suggests a folded paper at least. Simple message outside, then more complex as you unfold. Test any proposed door-to-door items – starting by pushing it through a difficult letterbox.

To whom is it to be delivered?

It may be all households within a 10-minute drive of a shop. For haircuts, about 5 kilometres is the furthest anyone will drive in a built up area, but this can extend up to 16 kilometres in extended suburban areas such as Greater Manchester. Research suggests 22 kilometres is the absolute limit. For pizzas, you know the distance you are prepared to deliver. A number of organizations will supply geodemographics to you, which profile areas. These organizations are listed in Appendix 3. They include CACI, Mosaic, Superprofiles and Define. Members of the DMA Door-to-door Council have access to a property classification that goes down to delivery level – that is in about 250 household blocks.

How will it be delivered?

The choice is between Royal Mail, local newspapers or specialist distribution companies. The Royal Mail offers specific days and has access to all the UK households. The item will be delivered with the post Local newspapers cover 86 per cent of the UK and deliver on specific days of the week. If the newspaper is part of the Audited Bureau of Circulation (ABC) Verified Free Newspaper Distribution (VFD) then you can check the circulation is as claimed.

If a specialist is used, it should be a member of the DMA Door-to-Door Council (formerly AHD) which agrees to operate by a monitored code of practice. The specialist offers two alternatives – solus or shared. Solus is when the item is delivered on its own, which gives greater impact but costs more. Solus can be further enhanced by combining it with a personal call – known as 'knock and drop' – where the deliverer knocks and asks questions for data collecting purposes at the same time as making the delivery.

Shared or omnibus deliveries are made with around four items delivered at the same time. The delivery time and date for shared door-to-door delivery may only be within a period of say three weeks.

What checks need to be made to validate delivery?

Specialist distributors will back-check post delivery for an extra fee, to report on the level of receipt and recall. Beyond that, research companies will need to be employed against a statistically representative sample and carry out interviews, probably wise for drops over 5 million. It is possible to ask a few people in the area that are known to you to confirm deliveries. The responses (if you ask for them) themselves will give an indication if your staff are trained to ask the right questions – 'May I take your post-code?'

Completing a voucher for redemption will also indicate whether the area has been covered. It is often possible physically to go and see if one particular area has been covered. You may be seeking callers to a call centre through publishing a telephone number. Here again the call centre can be used to validate delivery. If the response is via a Web site, again it is possible through some part of the registration process to check how the browser was directed to the Web site.

It may be wise to confirm from some addresses in the targeted area that the material has been delivered. Also check that there are no piles of material sitting in heaps on street corners.

Tips

1. Judith Donovan's tip is to use a normal envelope for door-to-door delivery and create an overprint on the envelope of a fake franking to make it seem like mail.
2. As you will not be addressing the envelope to an individual, you need some form of salutation that is upbeat. This should give a clue as to the contents – 'Dear Cinderella, a magic new cleaner is here to take the drudgery out of chores...' Wax lyrical!
3. Just studying an appropriate scale map can give an indication of the type of houses in any area.

Accountability: setting and measuring key performance indicators

The purpose of the door-to-door delivery will, to an extent, determine what to measure. This is different from validation, which just checks that the activity has happened.

If the purpose is to provide customers for a database then the achievement may be a quantity, a number of names. If it is to increase covers in a restaurant then an offer – such as a free glass of wine with a meal on presentation of the voucher – will indicate how successful the activity has been. If the customers return to the restaurant in sufficient numbers thereafter (exceeding your set target), it will have been a success – but you need to track the customers and how much they generate for profit to find out whether you have covered the cost of the door-to-door activity.

You may be trying to get customers to call a telephone number or visit a Web site. In each case, the initial source of door-to-door needs to be found from the customer.

Successful achievement is measured by an increase in sales activity in the outlets to which the customer was directed. The level of successful achievement may include a measurement of ongoing repeat sales, as a result of customer bonding to your concept – product/service. This will almost certainly require further marketing activity as a follow up. The response to these too should be measured.

The number of voucher-accompanied purchases can indicate that customers understood, believed and valued the offer suffi- cient to make a purchase. Any follow up marketing activity, say direct mail or a telemarketing call, to those responding, may further enhance sales but the results in each case should be measured.

Return of the redeemed vouchers from retail outlets can supply information about the purchaser's address for further marketing activity. A surge in product or service purchases or enquiries, or from increased orders placed by retailers, should confirm the success or at least greater interest in the product or service.

Key performance indicator measurement

Measure orders placed over a period of time from before the door- to-door drop was made. Measure the percentage of vouchers redeemed. Measure identified calls to the call centre; registrations on a Web site.

Use CACI research material for the area to compare your take up by that area and with your customer profile. It might allow more careful door-to-door targeting in any future door-to-door marketing activity. Measure cost of marketing activity versus target. Measure the effect on profit.

What costs will be involved in door-to-door delivery?

There is the cost of the door-to-door delivery and the cost of print and production. These costs will be given in £s per thousand. They will vary depending on the size/weight of the door-to-door delivery, whether it is solus or shared.

There is the cost of the logistics and management of the operation including clearance of the design. Finally, there is the cost of coupon redemption or data capture and retailer handling fees. Targeting costs and research costs would be additional.

Code of practice and the law

See the DMA Code of Practice – in Chapter 4.

Associated topics

Direct Mail – see Chapter 4 for ideas on what might be put in a package and the creative design.
Call centres – see Chapter 12 for telephone responses and Chapter 5 for Web site contact.

10

Leaflets and handouts

WHAT ARE LEAFLETS AND HANDOUTS?

Leaflets are printed material usually placed in dispensers readily available to customers at places where the customer is likely to pass. Handouts are printed material placed directly into the hands of the customer by people handing out the material, usually where there is a high footfall of potential customers.

Dispensers of leaflets are widely used in the travel and tourist trade in hotels near the reception/entry/ticket purchase/hall area. At exhibitions, they can be placed within the carrier bag supplied at registration or entry. In towns, leaflets can be placed under windscreens of appropriate makes of car.

At mainline railway stations handouts can substantially increase the numbers diverting to a stand on the concourse where not every person passes by on their way to and from platforms to exits. Where a venue is not ordinarily in use as a retail outlet, handouts can entice people in. Examples are the use of town halls for the sale of art or craft items where some form of publicity is needed to draw attention to a retail event going on inside. There are benefits to placing a leaflet inside your product – see below.

The advantages of leaflets and handouts

Leaflets and handouts can draw attention to:

■ a new outlet or new attraction;

- ▓ an existing attraction;
- ▓ a new product or service;
- ▓ a product or service with a limited availability;
- ▓ a specific exhibition stand.

The leaflet or handout needs to thought out carefully and the purpose thought through.

Leaflets

The leaflet may offer an incentive to encourage a visit or patronage. For an attraction, it needs to spell out clearly what is on offer. On the Swanage Railway on the Isle of Purbeck in Dorset, people assumed that no food was available on the trains and made other arrangements – the leaflet only indicated on the *timetable* that a buffet car was available. Only railway buffs knew the appropriate symbols. The leaflet now spells out food availability: the refreshment takings on the Railway are now a significant contribution to revenue.

For an attraction, the leaflet needs to spell out clearly what is on offer. Distribution is important to consider – it is easy to leave this to chance – but unwise. Where a dispenser of leaflets is used, hotels, information centres and attractions often have their own dispenser banks and the leaflet should match the size of the dispenser. In a retail outlet a dispenser may need to be provided – these should be heavily customized – or do not be surprised to find other leaflets placed in true 'cuckoo' fashion. Supplies of leaflet refills and re-stocking arrangements need to be made, particularly when the leaflet details go out of date.

If the leaflet is used for an existing attraction, it can be a conversation starter to build a customer relationship when the customer visits the attraction or redeems the incentive. For example on the Swanage Railway inquiries found people were travelling daily from as far afield as Nottingham to visit the attraction. Leaflet placings previously had been based on the assumption that day-trippers would travel no further than from the M4 corridor. Visitors to that attraction enjoy talking about the Railway often in nostalgic terms and volunteer staff are made aware of this.

A leaflet at an exhibition can be used to build a database with space available to enter name, address, etc, if it is to be used as a voucher for say subscriptions to trade magazines or for an offer of a demonstration at a site away from the exhibition. Subsequent marketing activity can then be applied to achieve sales.

Leaflets put on car windscreens offering car valeting, MOTs, garaging and servicing are quite commonplace. Check on the weather before placing; if there is imminent danger of rain do not be surprised if the response to your sodden leaflet is very low.

Handouts

A handout at an exhibition can be used to attract people to a stand offering a prize draw. There is no need for such a handout to ask for names and addresses. To obtain names and addresses of those visiting an exhibition stand it is common practice to call for business cards to be placed in a receptacle with the incentive of an entry into a daily prize draw. (Barcode readers of the name tag can achieve the same.)

Product leaflets

A leaflet placed in a product can provide 'free' product market research or it can be used to build a database of customers for customer panels, future direct mailings. Place a questionnaire inside your product. People will fill it in and send it to you. The response is enhanced if you invite them to enter a free prize draw. You will be amazed at the numbers that respond.

Analyse the information for new product development and attitude and awareness purposes. Responses to where they purchase will indicate preferred distributors and areas of the country where your target market is strong. Offer through a coupon – even printed onto the packaging – a product support leaflet (menus, methods of alternative use). People will volunteer information. You have names and addresses – ask them if they agree to you retaining them for further product information, joining future customer panels – then you can place their names and addresses on a database.

Handouts and leaflets as a part of integrated marketing

The distribution of leaflets or giving out handouts can enhance some other marketing activity in a local area. Leaflets provide basic awareness reminders of a concept at an appropriate distribution point. Handouts are particularly useful for a launch of a concept or the opening of a new outlet.

MAKING LEAFLETS OR HANDOUTS WORK

The leaflets/handouts need to be designed, printed and distributed at the appropriate time. Check your marketing objective; leaflets and handouts will probably be an activity within a campaign, supporting the opening of a retail outlet, attendance at a stand at an exhibition.

Leaflets

A leaflet has to match the distribution outlet requirement. This may well limit it to a three-fold A4 size or folded multiples of that. Research carefully the most appropriate outlets for the leaflets to be distributed and displayed. Look at plenty of examples of leaflets – particularly competitive offerings. Be really different! A leaflet without an incentive may well be rapidly discarded.

Handouts

As for door-to-door delivery the message should be short and simple – like a poster, perhaps with an incentive. Design the handout as a mini poster so that people can rapidly absorb what the message and/or offer is. It should then give brief clear instructions as to how to carry out the message and or redeem the offer. It should be 'special', entitling the holder of the handout to an immediate benefit. Remember if your concept is worthwhile, most people will buy more than just the offer; indeed customers accept that the offer may be dependent on another purchase.

Tips

1. You may need clearance to operate any leaflet distribution on premises such as railway stations. There is a charge for using some large station concourses.
2. It will be easy to measure the numbers of leaflets handed out by people by recording how many boxes/part boxes of leaflets they consume.
3. The people handing out the information offer a billboard surface. Consider repeating your leaflet message on their clothing. T-shirts are easy to have printed with your message. It also gives a greater provenance to the leaflet.

Accountability: setting and measuring key performance indicators

The purpose of the leaflet will govern the achievement measurement. Some form of yardstick may be needed to measure the impact of the leaflet. You may need to carry out market research into the perceptions and attitudes generated by the leaflet.

For leaflets used for awareness that are taken from dispensers, staff at an attraction need to be trained to ask how people heard about the attraction and if through a leaflet, where they found the leaflet and enter a simple form with the response. This will measure both the effectiveness of leaflet distribution as a marketing activity in promoting purchases. This is made easier when the potential customer redeems the leaflet offer; this prompts the staff to start the recording process.

The leaflet can be used to extract information from the customer (name and address minimum). The opportunity should not be missed to use the information to start a customer relationship, hopeful of future referral or repeat business. So recording names and addresses for a future marketing activity should not be discarded lightly.

If the leaflet is designed to persuade people just to have a look and merely note new premises or a new retail outlet, where you only want to increase awareness, visitors may be counted entering using a click counter (hand-operated or electronic). You need to record attendance before the leaflet was offered; to track any changes consequent upon the leaflet.

Key performance indicator mechanisms

Collection of redeemed vouchers and their analysis needs to be organized. The distribution of leaflets and quantities supplied needs to be recorded. Measure the percentage redemption. Measure the cost of marketing activity versus target. Measure the effect on profit.

What costs will be involved for leaflets and handouts?

The costs of design and printing, the costs of research and distribution to leaflet dispensers, the cost of employing persons to hand out the material.

Code of practice and the law

For the DMA Code of Practice see Chapter 4.

11

Mail order

WHAT IS MAIL ORDER?

Mail order makes available to customers a selection of the same items that are available in the store. The items are displayed in a mail order brochure and can be ordered through an order form included with the brochure. There is a blurring of the distinction between mail order and catalogue. Perhaps mail order might now be more appropriately described as a selection of items of what is available to purchase. A catalogue includes every item and is normally supplied by a firm with no retail outlets.

The Next Directory led the mail order revolution in 1988, taking over the Grattan list. Next is a chain of retail clothing shops. The Next initiative helped break the mould that mail order was only for the 'working class'. A plethora of upmarket and specialist mail order products have been launched since, eg Lands End, Orbis, Racing Green, Hawkshead and Boden who operate in the clothing market, while The White Company brings a niche offering of household lines and goods with the distinguishing feature that they are all white. There are books (Book Club Associates) and CD/video (Britannia) mail order companies. Each book and CD/video mail order company offers a different selection each month to those signed up.

Some stores such as Argos and Ikea produce catalogues of everything they sell, but the items are normally purchased from the store. For businesses, office stationery companies, such as Viking (now also on the Internet), Strakers, Neat Ideas, and others, offer mail order to the business client.

Online shopping supported by an offline catalogue is found to be extremely successful. There are plenty of examples in the business sector, such as PC World (also going for the home market), Jungle, Global Direct, Misco for computers and peripherals.

There are also catalogues of catalogues on the Internet, 'such as www.Pricerunner.com, making price comparisons between suppliers both off- and online. A special feature is that customers can get added value and add value themselves by commenting on the products in the catalogues.

DMA research shows that the same percentages across all life stages use mail order/catalogue shopping. It is not as popular as retail therapy – 'just going round the shops'. One of the main points of resistance to mail order is stated as 'delivery times not being convenient'.

The advantages of mail order

Mail order can extend the reach of a business to more customers. Small single outlet stores can enhance their sales by adding mail order. Specialist gift shops, secondhand book shops (offering first editions), model railway shops, indeed any specialist niche outlet should consider offering mail order to its customers.

The decision to offer mail order should not be taken lightly, because it requires a commitment to customers in terms of providing them with information and a quality of delivery. The logistics can be quite demanding, preparing orders, packaging and dispatching items, sending out pro forma invoices, collecting payments and chasing bad debts. A reliable and 'competitive on price' delivery/distribution service must be in place. There is a need for a system and operation to be able to accept back products found to be faulty or not required.

For many business-to-business suppliers (serving those in the retail trade for example) their marketing activities consist of having an exhibition stand at a number of trade exhibitions up and down the country at which orders are taken, which are then topped up through mail order for the rest of the year. Customers then order over the telephone from a brochure/catalogue (with a price list) and receive occasional mail shots with special offers to tempt them to order more. Mail order is becoming a major marketing activity. A number of firms now offer a Web site alternative for placing orders.

A brochure from an Internet Web site is Figleaves, which went to 130,000 prospects and achieved a response rate of 4.7 per cent. A 16-page flyer was subsequently sent out via the customer database and 3,900 orders resulted. The latest 64-page catalogue was distributed to 200,000 people with a 3.4 per cent response rate. Figleaves Chairman, Daniel Nabarro, says 'The visual and tactile qualities of our catalogue comes across better in print than on screen. Direct mail pushes people to the site and gives them a call to action, but sending the requested catalogue gives them a catalogue to peruse without the need to boot up.'

Mail order as a part of integrated marketing

Mail order is almost always additional to normal marketing activities. A campaign may consist of some advertisements in an area – probably extending the area of a retail outlet – followed by a direct mailshot in the same area, followed by telemarketing with two follow up mailings to those who do not respond initially.

Examples of this sort of approach might include sales of cases of better-than-average wine (ie more highly priced) to people who are likely to drink wine regularly and are likely to have the appropriate income (and probably live in an upmarket area). The benefits are that regular customers once hooked are likely to provide an assured income stream.

MAKING MAIL ORDER WORK

The objective – the purpose of the mail order marketing activity – should be borne in mind all the time. Usually it is to supplement your retail activity or Internet activity, often supplying regular and valued customers with a tangible and convenient reminder of your products. It saves the journey. Remember that 22 kilometres is a researched limit of travel, so send mail order to those who live further away. Remember that research also shows sales increase if you support a Web site with a brochure. Think carefully about meeting the six Cs, especially convenience and cost. Then consider:

▨ The scale of the mail order service you want to offer. Is it going to be everything you stock (ie a catalogue operation – see Chapter 7) or a limited range of items?

▓ How is the limited range of items to be varied, and how often? Plan several brochures ahead.

▓ You also need to think of the operation of your mail order service – a fulfilment operation effectively (see Chapter 6).

▓ You will need to develop packaging and delivery that works. You should expect customers to be irate if you do not deliver within 28 days. (The DMA Code of Practice requires members to deliver within 30 days.)

▓ Are you going to allow free post and packaging above a certain order value? (Viking offers this for orders above £30.)

▓ What is your policy going to be on people wishing to return the goods?

▓ You may wish to set a minimum order value.

▓ How are people going to pay? Cheque, cash order or credit card? Merchant services are provided by high street banks, allowing people to pay you by credit card. They take a certain percentage of the value of the order. They may refuse you if you have no track record of trading. They may also refuse if they assess the value of the goods to be too small. Your policy on returns and your ability to return the goods may affect their decision. There are certain Internet-based bank services that are far less demanding on credit card ordering but take a higher percentage. If you are using the Internet, you should provide security for credit card users.

You will need to cost the whole activity to see that you make money on the operation. If you are a small firm, then start small and offer only a 'cheques with order' service. Do not dispatch the order until the cheque has been cleared. Test the mail order service. Do it in-house initially. Limit the customers to whom you offer it – say, only to those who live further away, but do spend a reasonable amount with you when they shop.

DIY, suppliers, agencies

Unlike a catalogue-based business where the very success of the business depends on the catalogue, with mail order, you can afford to make mistakes and learn and DIY is possible. However, using an expert for the first issue is probably very wise to avoid basic oversights. If you are using an agency, employ a firm that has produced and printed brochures and/or catalogues before and insist on seeing examples.

Production of the mail order brochure

Once you have decided to go ahead, then there is the question of producing your brochure, sheets, catalogue, pricing list, order form. Taking those items you have selected for mail order, how you are to present them is key to success.

Look at a broad range of mail order devices by competitors and others. Look also at CD ROMs and video as alternatives to print. Particularly consider presentation – paper quality, weight, feel – do your customers have PCs? Remember the feel and weight (and smell) will affect the customer, as will the presentation itself.

How legible is the print to be? Older people probably only see a font size of 12pt or larger. Older people over 70 may not have access to PCs (though the author's mother at age 86 has e-mail).

It is wise to test the mail order component parts rigorously. Is the mail order device showing off the items well? (See Chapter 7 for more detailed thoughts on catalogue production.) Photographs of appropriate settings of the products in use will assist an understanding of what a product is for and suggest how it might be used/worn or placed. You can use duplex printing yourself to test the brochure. Such printers now cost little more than ordinary printers. The design of the order form itself (see Chapter 7) can affect sales. Make it easy to use. If there are relatively few items and your customer database is limited, then you may be able to produce the mail order brochure entirely in-house. For a test brochure use quality photographs on quality paper. Sticking real photographs on to the sheets is better than poor photocopies.

Tips

1. Do not re-invent the wheel, use the expertise of others – see how other firms lay out their mail order pages with photographs, codes and pricing of the items, and as for catalogues see how a customer is taken through the process of ordering and the layout of the order form, see how the catalogue is sectioned, introduced, indexed and where the guarantee is placed.

2. Once you have a successful mail order brochure keep it in digital format so that it is easy to amend and re-create. Your customers will appreciate finding items in the same place each issue.

3. An alternative for photographs is to digitally print out photographs with your message and then laminate the result. This provides the glossy look and an expensive feel.

4. Keep a full record of mail order purchases and your normal sales. You can often use a mail order 'special offer' to clear an item nearing the end of its lifecycle.

5. Keep a full record of all items returned as 'damaged' or broken and particularly where orders fail to arrive. Helmsmen client experience shows that it is only a few who are regular 'returners' of damaged goods and – assuming you have your packaging, dispatch and delivery operating well – you can point out this fact to them. Eventually, do not trade with them. The same applies to cheques not being honoured. (Helmsmen client experience when trading B2B is about a 0.3 per cent loss per year. The firms who do a runner should be recorded and their names passed on to other companies trading in the sector – you meet them at exhibitions etc. Also inform trading associations.)

6. Always use pro forma invoices for first orders. Watch for the scam of a small first mail order, which is paid in full, followed by a large second order that is to be paid after receipt. Either ask for cash on delivery or split it into many little orders with each delivery after payment of the previous one or you may find the customer has done a runner.

7. Be aware of overseas firms offering to establish trade in their countries from samples that you provide them. Ensure their bona fide existence first (through the embassy/high commission).

8. Ensure when sending any items overseas you have built into your products measures that are difficult to copy. (Helmsmen's engineering expertise is used by clients to produce designs that are difficult to copy without expensive capital investment – this helped in one case to put a competitor out of business, as it could not achieve the quality when copying the design).

9. For a reasonably bona fide overseas business, if you feel you cannot service the territory by mail order, why not offer a franchise or licence to produce. On one visit to India, a UK home safety product was being manufactured as a direct copy, but without a franchise or under licence, as the UK firm had universally decided not to let anyone else produce its products. In this case it could neither manage nor supply the Indian market nor actually achieve the lower price the Indian manufacturer could achieve. The Indian business in this case would have been happy to pay the licence and could have supplied the UK at a price offering greater profitability.

10. Test every mail order brochure in every way. A misprinted postcode or telephone number can cost you dear. Be aware of changes in telephone numbers that are forecast. Also check with senior management for foreknowledge of any mergers or changes in trading name. In recent years, a number of firms have been caught out with piles of useless catalogues or having to print errata slips or paste over incorrect names and contacts.

Accountability: setting and measuring key performance indicators

The process to achieve mail order customers may take time and when set against actual cost of the marketing activities, in the short term may show a loss. It is better to profile customers and look to match the profile of new customers.

Key performance indicator mechanisms

The eventual measure of achievement is regular and valuable customers. Measure actual increase and percentage increase in numbers of customers. Record over time whether new customers achieve regular and valuable customer status. Measure cost of marketing activity versus target. Measure the effect on profit.

What costs will be involved for mail order?

There are the costs of managing the operation – taking orders, packaging and dispatch, delivery and the associated paperwork – delivery, accounting and financial.

There are the costs associated with providing customer services, complaints, warranty, returns and the financial accounting (credit notes, refunds).

There are the costs associated with the production of the brochure (planning, photography, layout, design, print and delivery). Remember the quality of the mail order device and its layout will to an extent set the buying feeling of the buyer as favourable or not.

There are the costs of the supporting advertising or direct marketing to launch and sustain the mail order operation.

Code of practice and the law

See the DMA Code of Practice, Chapter 4.

12

Call centres and telemarketing

WHAT ARE CALL CENTRES?

A call centre is a telephone service, responding to or making telephone calls. A call centre is nowadays both an inbound and outbound service, whereas telemarketing is outbound. Margaret Allen in 1997 forecast that by the end of the decade, call centres would exceed £2 billion turnover a year. She was right. The DMA census gives the figure for 1999/2000 as £2.419 billion.

A call centre can be in-house or outsourced. This is usually the first decision a company has to make. The decision should be based on how near to the core of your business the call centre is: for a telephone bank it is a core service. If it is an additional activity then it is probably better outsourced. Firms such as BPS Teleperformance have been operating call centres for years and can give guidance on expected call rates, lengths of call, peak call times and conversion rates. Their experience means they are fairly accurate at predicting likely response rates.

Where a call centre is outsourced, call centre staff can be trained to appear to be a part of your firm. They are able to increase the number of people answering calls should a surge arise and divert calls to other call centres if the demand goes beyond that.

Call centres should be notified of marketing activity dates when the target audience is to be 'hit'. Call centre staff log all calls and provide both the log and an analysis of the data collected in a variety of formats for each period (typically a week) and compare each week with every previous week.

Call centre operators operate with a tree-form pre-agreed script obtaining information from the caller, passing information to the caller during the call, as well as responding with appropriate information on request.

Automated systems or partial automation can help direct calls to an appropriate team within the call centre. Customers are quite happy to give a name and address to an automated system for a brochure request. Voice recognition can assist in transposing this to data for a database and subsequently provide a mailing list. If the customer has been given a unique number with a mailshot they can key this on request to simplify the automation process. Any automated system has limitations; all the research indicates that customers prefer dealing with a real person.

Buying an appropriate machine allows a small firm to have seemingly many extensions. People perceive you are larger when multiple choices are offered when their call is answered. This can be helpful to separate sales calls from queries about maintenance, when a salesperson calls in to take their calls. This opportunity to automate needs to be balanced against the irritation of customers if the process takes too long.

The advantages of call centres

It is a cost-effective way of providing a professionally trained response to customer callers. Customers can be either existing or potential, business customers or consumers. It can provide customer care, customer service, act as the follow up to direct response (TV, radio, poster or press). A call centre can make sales calls.

The call centre brief should be clear about the objectives. For direct response, the database of interested potential customers is most useful to both you and any involved suppliers.

Careful consideration of the order and content of call centre responses allowing flexibility of response makes customers perceive that they are leading the conversation while actually having information extracted from them to meet the objectives.

For a Helmsmen client, the call centre staff obtained information regarding where the caller had seen the telephone number, the caller's name, address and postcode, the time and date of call, and gave out information giving the name and telephone number of their nearest supplier and an alternative. The call centre staff were pre-briefed about the client product and were able to answer general queries as required. The telephone number appeared in editorials, advertisements, inserts, mailshots and on the Web site. The supplier subsequently redeemed a voucher offer.

The telephone line itself may be offered as a free phone or local call line rather than a national call charge line to encourage prospective callers to make the call. The call centre will have a number of lines available that can be used – it is important to get the number right in all marketing material. The call centre can take orders. It can be used to confirm that other marketing activities have happened as agreed.

Outbound telemarketing is more successful with B2B than with consumers. A call is accepted if it is seen to be relevant and offers a clear benefit to the customer. It can be used to fix appointments, even when near cold calling, if the relevance and benefit measures are readily understood. It is better if it is part of a campaign and the recipient has already been sent direct mail and been told to expect a call. It can be used as a customer relationship-building tool routinely calling customers to check all is well, to find out what is selling, to take ideas for new products, obtain feedback about consumer interest in purchases of your concept, to take orders or make sales offers.

Call centres as a part of integrated marketing

An inbound call centre is a part of integrated marketing and must be consistent with other marketing activities. An outbound call centre (telemarketing) could theoretically act entirely on its own but it is wisest to integrate it in a campaign, where typically, a letter precedes the telephone call and, on success, a letter confirming the call outcome follows.

A campaign may consist of some advertisements in an area followed by a direct mail shot in the same area followed by telemarketing with two follow up mailings to those who do not respond initially.

When call centres have a strategic role

A call centre used in its telemarketing role can be a means to carry out research with existing customers to ascertain views or new concept acceptability. It is a fast means of obtaining a response. It should not be used to carry out market research without training the operators in marketing – particularly the ability to pick up what is not normally articulated. Training is required to overcome the natural instinct to please and give answers the person called thinks match the need.

MAKING A CALL CENTRE OPERATION WORK

Whether you decide to undertake the operation in-house (in which case you will have recruited persons with the necessary expertise) or you use a call centre (see Appendix 3) the need to clear your mind as to what you are trying to do is paramount.

Think of the marketing purpose throughout as given in the marketing objective. Produce a call centre brief, which conveys:

▦ the campaign objectives and the purpose of the call centre marketing activity within that campaign;
▦ a description of the target audience;
▦ any responses that are required, collection of what data, etc;
▦ estimates of response rate (immediacy of calls is a factor with direct response TV; radio and press are more even and often it is several repeats or re-readings before a call centre is contacted);
▦ whether a freephone, local or national or special tariff rate is to be applied;
▦ the success criteria;
▦ details of any test of the operational procedures;
▦ campaign dates.

Agree a script with the call centre – usually in a 'tree' format. Test the script. After say a week's operation, call a meeting and obtain feedback. How well does the script work, what changes are suggested? Test changes and repeat. See below for Code of Practice.

DIY, suppliers, agencies

An in-house (DIY) operation is recommended where it is not a core part of the operation. First-time users are advised to use a supplier until the call centre service operation is fully understood before taking the operation in-house.

Tips

1. Visit the call centre and explain and demonstrate the concept to the teams, with product samples. It is important to train the call centre in your company. This rarely happens from discussions with call centre staff. Helmsmen have taken products to call centres on behalf of clients with really beneficial results. Product demonstrations give an understanding of your products, which can be used when the call centre staff talk to your potential customers. It is a motivator to the call centre staff to see the products they are taking calls about.
2. For a small firm, if you want to seem like a larger organization than you are, then the purchase of some of the latest telephone answering machines might solve the problem.
3. Use a 'professional' voice to enhance answering machine tapes.
4. In Helmsmen's experience, call centre managers have a vast experience of handling campaigns and will describe total failures from top blue-chip companies and runaway successes from others. They are full of excellent advice on how best to use their services. The good call centre operators will not rip you off, rather they want to see you succeed and give advice that is pragmatic and helpful; a successful telemarketing/call centre operation brings repeat business and enhances their reputation.
5. It is important that the script the call centre uses matches your brand values.

Accountability: setting and measuring key performance indicators

Let the call centre know what you have set as the key performance indicators. Experience indicates they will probably be able to tailor the measurements they use to meet what you want measured.

Usually a response target is set. The call centre managers have experience and can advise of the likely response. This may be no more than a return of the calls resulting from a direct mail shot. Promotions and voucher redemption may increase the response numbers.

A call centre can be used as an intermediate measurement for a number of activities. For example, the measurement of the number of customers actually redeeming vouchers at suppliers was the target for one marketing activity – there was a correlation between take-up and supplier distance from customer. This correlation exercise was achieved using call centre data. A review of distribution resulted and additional suppliers were found to improve national coverage.

Key performance indicator mechanisms

Modern telephone exchanges often have facilities to store details of all calls made in and out – alternatively a detailed statement can be ordered. This is a source of additional and sometimes valuable information on the performance of any marketing activity that uses a telephone line.

Measuring the differing response levels to different marketing activities all linked through a call centre can be a helpful and cost-effective way of assessing achievement. Call centre staff can assist with suggestions.

Call centre logs should provide data as agreed. Analysis of the data will allow measurements such as regional interest, perception as to price and value, comprehension or otherwise of the product or service offered.

Call centres measure other marketing activities. Call records analysis can confirm that an advertising regional insert has indeed gone to a region. Measure the cost of marketing activity versus target.

What costs will be involved in call centres and telemarketing?

The contract is usually a mix of a fixed fee for management and set up charges and an operational per call fee. First-time customers will be asked to pay a deposit up front to cover costs, which is refunded if the call levels are not achieved.

Code of practice and the law

A DMA Code of Practice exists for call centre operations. Disclosure of the company name and any third party must be made to the recipient; the calls must be honest (not masquerading as research when they are sales calls); the calls must be made at reasonable hours, conducted with courtesy and procedures to allow the customer to withdraw at any time or call back and cancel. Finally, numbers called must not be at random but follow an agreed list following the Telephone Preference Service rules. (The Telephone Preference Service is voluntary and enables customers to register their telephone number if they do not wish to receive sales telephone calls through a freephone number. The service is paid for by firms who are given access to the list and saves them wasting time on telesales calls to unreceptive customers. Note there is also a similar mailing preference service, which conversely allows encouragement of preferred sales mailings if requested.) See also Chapter 4.

Associated topic

Customer relationship marketing (CRM)

CRM is an amalgam of database marketing, customer relations and (key) account management. The coming of age of the mobile phone, the Internet and IT capability (that is, computers operating with enough speed and memory capacity) and a better grasp of knowledge management (supplying just the information required when it is needed and in a comprehensible form) have made CRM take off. In essence, CRM allows you to:

■ increase market share;
■ reduce the costs of customer management;
■ recruit new, high quality customers in a more targeted fashion;
■ defend and retain existing customers, reducing the cost of sales;
■ develop more value out of existing customers long term and in profitability;
■ protect companies against riskier customers.

The latest book on *Successful Customer Relationship Marketing* is just out by Brian Foss and Merlin Stone (published by Kogan Page). Customer Relationship Marketing, another excellent book in this series on this subject, which is already into its second edition. Published by Kogan Page it is written by Merlin Stone, Neil Woodcock and Liz Machtynger.

CRM is defined (by Merlin Stone *et al*) as 'The use of a wide range of marketing (including field marketing), communication, service and customer care approaches to: identify a company's named individual customers, create a relationship between the company and its customers that stretches over many transactions and manage that relationship to the benefit of the customers and the company'. In other words, CRM finds you the customer, gets to know you, keeps in touch with you, tries to ensure you get what you want from a company in every aspect of a company's dealings with you, checks that you are getting what you were promised and overall it is mutually worthwhile to both the customer and the company.

CRM is particularly good at recognizing the stage of the buying process that a customer has reached. Few customers make quick leaps from prospect to loyal customer to lost customer. The CRM process also allows the level of relationship to match that required by the customer. The book, having looked at the customer and the customer's needs, then looks at the company and how to develop contact strategies. Key to CRM success is training people within the company to deliver CRM. The book covers technology and e-CRM.

Director magazine reports that a recent survey found that 67 per cent of customers go elsewhere because nobody has kept in touch with them. It is important to keep in touch with them. The report goes on to say, 'Remember it costs six times as much to get a new customer than to keep an existing one. Follow up a sale or a completion of service by asking your customer if they are happy with it and if there is anything else you can do for them'. Unfortunately the UK tends to have a customer culture of silence: that is, rather than being vocal people tend to complain with their feet and go elsewhere. Unless you make the effort to ask why, you could lose those customers forever.

The author has experience of this, now refusing any service of a communications provider who has never been in touch to ask why the author ceased to use the provider.

So what can a business do to keep in touch? To find out all about your service and how customers view it, use a marketing consultant routinely to carry out a sample client survey for up to say 500 customers. Use mystery shoppers (see Chapter 13) for customers servicing a large number of consumers. For more than 500 customers you may need structured market research to find out. The remedy though is to apply CRM alongside the marketing consultant, market research or mystery shopper activity.

Clearly, anyone contemplating using a call centre or indeed undertaking any direct marketing activity, needs to have a grasp of CRM. The subject is a book in itself. The Stone et al book is readily available. It demonstrates how to implement CRM.

Other associated topics
For information on catalogues see Chapter 7.
For lists, see Chapter 4.

13

Field marketing

WHAT IS FIELD MARKETING?

Field marketing, as it is now known, includes direct selling, exhibitions and roadshows, merchandising, auditing, sampling and demonstration, mystery shopping. It can be differentiated because it is *face-to-face personal contact* direct marketing. Field marketing is also measured strictly in terms of results.

Field marketing can operate in a consumer environment (whether at a retail site or at home), business environment or a mix of both. It can operate at any level from local to international. It can be both an in-house activity or outsourced. The benefit of outsourcing is that the supplier of field marketing staff has experience, knowledge and professional skill. For example, supplied exhibition staff are probably familiar with most exhibition venues. Suppliers of field marketing staff can probably react more quickly to time; that is, to meet short-term needs and to react effectively to any constraints that are imposed and they are usually managed by equally professional and experienced persons.

There are some 30 companies in the UK, according to the DMA, offering to undertake outsourced sales and promotional activities, employing about 15,000 staff and acting as agents for a number of firms. This may make greater sense as it saves on many salespeople visiting the same customers. The weakness, where a single person agency is operating, is that the salesperson will be inclined to sell more of the products from the firm that remunerates at a higher rate or whose products are easiest to sell – agents tend to optimize their effort to obtain the highest return overall. Occasionally, salespeople employed by competing firms will combine and visit mutual customers on behalf of all to save their own time. For example, cigarette and tobacco product salespeople from competing organizations may meet at a motorway service station and then visit confectionery, tobacconist and newspaper (CTN) outlets on behalf of all of them. This collusion depends on the individual salesperson's beliefs; arrangements such as this only flourish with consenting salespeople and in an environment of 'poor' supervision if the practice is not condoned.

Direct selling (field marketing sales) is when the salesperson visits the customer at their premises or at a place other than their own premises. The purpose of the visit is to close a sale and refresh and build on the relationship. Direct selling people are equipped with product presenters, order forms and new products to demonstrate. They may occasionally take stock to sell or deliver. Customer relationships can be developed and 'bonding' develops between the direct selling person and the buyer. This bonding is difficult to break and order-taking is assured, particularly for new products introduced. It is a traditional way of making sales. It is also expensive.

In the retail sector, the use of 'mystery shoppers' is recognized as an effective way of testing if the concept is properly being sold – particularly for services or a service/product mix. Mystery shoppers can be the means to reward and motivate staff where service beyond the standard set is observed. A number of agencies offer a mystery shopper service. Include in the mystery shopper reports any of the range of service items you want checked. *Director* magazine reports that between £25 million and £40 million is spent annually on mystery shopping in the UK to facilitate objective feedback for management on standards of service and customer care.

Demonstrations and sampling, exhibition and roadshow staff provide the resource for their respective event types. They provide the opportunity to increase sales, gauge customer reaction and raise the profile of products. Demonstrations and sampling are often set up in retail sites – particularly for food and drink items.

Merchandisers combine sales with customer relations; they refill and re-stock sales plans on behalf of customers often visiting many outlets of the same customer chain within an area. Merchandising also ensures space is well utilized, presentation is both up to standard and consistent, and displays comply with any promotional needs. Merchandisers are often the front line in fighting for space on customer's shelves. Merchandisers provide feedback on the customer and direct selling staff.

Field marketing staff often have the best insight into customers' and clients' objectives, the way they operate and an understanding of any critical client timings. This insight should be harvested.

Auditors look at competitors' and your own products, prices, availability, customer service or anything with which they are tasked.

Merchandisers, mystery shoppers, auditors and direct selling persons usually work to a pre-arranged schedule of visits based either on area or customer categorization. The schedule will have been confirmed by a series of telephone calls (except for mystery shoppers). Occasionally a telephone call may replace a visit but the personal contact and personal benefits that a visit bestows, building on customer relationships, by for example, taking a customer out to lunch and taking customer viewpoint feedback, are not foregone lightly. For the direct selling person, a mix of salary and commission or scale of salary increments based on sales achievement will influence their methods and achievement. In addition to salary and commission, direct selling people claim expenses relating to travel, often based on mileage travelled, and time-based subsistence payments for food, drink and accommodation. The DMA produces a best practice guideline for field marketing. See Appendix 3.

The advantages of field marketing

The prime purpose is to achieve sales – and substantially more sales than without field marketing. This is because of the relatively greater cost of field marketing than other direct marketing alternatives.

Traditionally, especially in business-to-business, but also for high value sales to consumers, or for high value consumers, salespeople have called on customers. Financial services products, which are complex to explain, fall into this category. The continuing use of salespeople to visit firms may be limited in future in some sales categories because of improving technology and the relatively high cost of such direct selling.

Field marketing is generally the most expensive of direct marketing alternatives because the cost of employing people is relatively greater. It should be used when other direct marketing activities cannot achieve a result. For example, where there is a need to demonstrate or explain a relatively complex concept or how a concept might be used. (Complexity has to be judged on a concept-by-concept basis. Very bright people are sometimes unable to grasp seemingly simple ideas.) Explaining complex concepts particularly applies to new concepts, especially those that are 'invisible' and/or rely on understanding mental processes.

Using a merchandiser is much more effective and reliable where a particular layout/re-stocking plan, which is known to catch the eye of the customer, is to be used in retail outlets and the cost of training all those in the re-stocking/layout plan is greater than one person visiting a number of sites.

The advent of the Internet has meant that it is possible to show considerable product ranges and product details, even demonstrating them with video clips to would-be buyers on a Web site. The Web buyer can add them to a virtual 'shopping basket' and place an order; Web sites now allow payment for goods online. The computer industry is, not surprisingly, fairly converted to Internet selling – supplementing the Web site sales with catalogue and call centre order taking. Surprisingly, some software programmes often require field marketing. Demo disks can often put across only a small part of what is available from software, a demonstration by a field marketing direct selling person is more powerful, particularly if they have found out from their audience the problems encountered that a new concept might solve.

Field marketing is not appropriate where salespeople have little perceived influence or actual input to the sale – commodity items, books, music are now becoming items that can be readily and successfully bought through the Internet. In addition, some firms produce their catalogues/brochures on CD ROM – with built-in Web ordering – if the PC is Web-enabled. In business, stationery items have become commodity items too, along with large ranges of tools, fixtures and fittings. The need for a salesperson as an intermediary can be dispensed with. New, complex concepts – products and or services – do still need a salesperson.

The known benefit of a salesperson's bonding with customers should not be forgotten or discarded lightly. Between large organizations where high value orders are sold and placed, 'key account managers' are the direct selling field marketing people.

In-house, you may have both sales and direct selling staff. 'Sales' is when people, typically in a retail situation, typically behind a counter and armed with a till, attempt to assist and persuade a potential customer to make a purchase or to trigger increased sales or to persuade sales of those concept items of higher bottom line value.

Direct selling is no longer geographically limited. Hong Kong tailors set up shop monthly in the UK hotels, sending reminders to existing customers and offer tailored suits, often made for a fraction of the UK cost. Equally, UK direct selling persons are found in every part of the globe.

Field marketing as a part of integrated marketing

Field marketing must be entirely integrated with all other marketing activities. This is best achieved though internal marketing. Field marketing staff need to be briefed on all other marketing activities. Equally, as a ready source of customer market research, their views should be sought.

When field marketing has a strategic role

The opinions and views of field marketing people should be sought whenever input is sought about customers. Equally, field marketing people could be used to try out new concepts on customers as part of their routine contact with customers. Auditors may also have some idea of what the competition is planning.

MAKING FIELD MARKETING WORK

Assume there is a requirement for field marketing; that is, the alternatives are assessed as unable to generate sufficient sales orders to meet the targets or the concept is too complex to put across other than using salespeople. If consideration to this has not been given, then review the need for field marketing.

As a start point, any field marketing person should generate more profit, bottom line, than the cost of employing them. This blinding flash of the obvious is often not adhered to, but is key to making money in a business. A direct salesperson or merchandiser should probably be handling orders of a value some 10 times more than the amount they are paid (assuming a reasonable profit margin – that is presuming an organization expects a return greater than that achieved by simply placing money in a savings account). This means that unless you have a turnover greater than £150,000 you probably should have no salespeople solely carrying out field marketing direct selling. In any case, there will be gaps if they are ill or away on holiday. At the other end of the scale, if a single customer is placing sufficient orders (£200,000+), then it may be helpful to appoint a key account manager for that customer to build the relationship so that a bond eventually forms. Then, for those customers that are not placing orders sufficiently large to warrant employing a key account manager, how can direct selling people best be organized? Before that is decided, do you outsource?

The decision to take is whether to carry out all or parts of field marketing in-house or to outsource. The same decision rationale with regard to using call centres should be applied. Is it a core activity? Is it required all year round? Does the direct selling require particularly commercially sensitive information? Consider in particular the management implications of managing the people if it is carried out in-house. Field marketing operations management is an intensive process requiring experience and the ability to manage and motivate people.

The target sales turnover needs to have the proportion of orders to be obtained by field marketing or field marketing as a part of a campaign set down (the remainder coming from existing customers' contracted orders, Internet sales, etc, who can be persuaded to buy through methods other than a direct selling person's visit). Deduct the key account managers' part. The remainder is the task of field marketing and how to organize that. Is the concept particularly complex to describe and sell to any sector or does any sector have any cultural or demographic peculiarities? If that is the case then specialist selling to that sector may be required and field marketing direct selling persons should be separately allocated to that task. Where there is no specialist sector selling and the direct selling operation can be generally applied then a geographic area assignment for direct selling is probably appropriate. Divide the area by principal access routes.

The allocation of field marketing direct selling operation is perhaps best described by examples. For a Helmsmen client supplier to the retail gift sector the primary meeting points with customers take place at a series of trade exhibitions in London, the Midlands, the North and in the West Country. Products can be seen and ordered and are 'sold' by direct selling field marketing exhibitors. The in-house team is supplemented by outsourced staff as required. Routine orders are taken over the phone by a small in-house call centre team , which also carries out telemarketing. Mail order catalogues are sent out to those who have difficulty in reaching outlets.

When carried out in-house it is important to fully integrate field marketing into a business. Field marketing people can easily consider themselves apart from and above other marketing persons.

Careful consideration of the methods to be employed and field marketing activities to be undertaken should take into account whether to divide customers geographically, by sector, by technical need or by organizational type.

Associated topic

Exhibitions/trade fairs

An exhibition is usually held separately for the trade and for customers. Sometimes there are trade-only days within a mixed exhibition. The difference is important in that the contact time is considerably different between the two types; typically of the order of one or two minutes' contact time only for customers – usually consumers – as against the trade, where typical contact time may be around 20 minutes. When Autotech, the trade exhibition for the Motor Industry, was first organized, manufacturers and suppliers assumed that the Motor Show parameters applied – stands manned by attractive scantily clad women dishing out glossy brochures. Now Autotech is manned by bright, chartered engineer women professionals with a full understanding of the highly technical products, capable of discussing matters for hours if needed.

Selling products is not allowed at exhibitions (for security among other reasons) but taking orders is often the key purpose. Exhibitions are generally held by trade and by category. Sometimes a number of categories are combined and held simultaneously such as for the spring and autumn fairs held at the NEC. An example of a single category exhibition is the toy trade fair held at the end of January, now at the Excel site in Docklands. The UK Toy Fair is one of four international toy fairs closely linked by succeeding dates when toys for the following year, but principally for Christmas, are displayed and orders taken.

Sometimes the majority of order taking for some categories is carried out at an exhibition – the early February spring fair is when most purchasing of calendars for the following year takes place. A new company selling calendars to the retail trade in the UK may only be able to find buyers prepared to order calendars at that exhibition almost to the exclusion of the rest of the year – with any ongoing sales sold to the same designs through merchandisers. The corollary is that to sell calendars widely in the UK will require attendance with a stand at the trade fair to take orders.

For every category there are one or more exhibitions held. To find out what exhibitions are held and where, there are specialist exhibition trade guides. The trade magazines and exhibition venues also list exhibitions held.

Exhibition stands are allowed on station concourses and shopping malls. These are usually arranged on a one-to-one basis between the station or mall operator and the exhibitor.

Not to be confused with exhibitions are shows, fairs (not just for trade), markets and car boot sales/garage sales. These are places where sales are allowed from stands. Some well-known exhibition venues are also used for shows and fairs, which may add to the confusion. There are also opportunities to sell to consumers at shows sponsored by the media – including TV – mimicking the Ideal Home Show sponsored by a newspaper (the *Daily Mail*). The BBC sponsors DIY, homemaking and fashion shows. There are a number of county shows and ones with a central attraction such as steam or agriculture or 'country themed' fairs. Markets are regular and often permanently established places where stalls/stands are available for hire controlled by councils or licensed operators (for example, Covent Garden, where a stall can be hired on a one day per week basis). Car boot sales allow members of the public sometimes alongside trade stalls to set up their own stands at regular sites. Garage sales are individual enterprises.

An exhibition can allow customers to handle, view, experience, sample, test, try, ask questions about and place orders for products and services. Careful selection of the exhibition (by category and trade) should ensure that plenty of the target market for your concept – products and services – will be attending. This does not mean that they will visit your stand or place orders – even if they have done so previously.

The design of the stand requires an understanding of the objectives set for attendance at the exhibition. The size and location within the exhibition area is important to consider as is stand-manning to cope with expected numbers. It is better to start small and learn from experience when considering stand size. If a part of the purpose is to understand customers' problems in detail and discuss possible product or service solutions then it may be important to include an area where there are limited distractions and a degree of perceived confidentiality. (Helmsmen suggest a particular design of booth that both hides and 'traps' the prospect, minimizes distractions and is relatively soundproof, yet allows an eye to be kept on the remainder of the stand by the stand person talking to the prospect. The booth has a small footprint.)

It is a good idea, if many brief discussions are likely to be required with prospective customers, to sit those manning that part of the stand on seats that place them at eye level with customers. This avoids fatigue. People are unhappy talking up or down to each other, preferring near horizontal eye contact. Areas of stand visible down aisles should have lettering large enough to be read at a distance with short crisp messages putting across concept benefits as 'attention getters'.

As a generalization based on observation both from attendance and stand manning over many years, most people on exhibition stands have received little or inappropriate training to 'sell' at exhibitions. Training can enhance the sales performance several times. (Helmsmen clients have increased order taking by a factor of three or four after training – the selling process at exhibitions is covered in Table 13.1. It is quite different from the normal sales process.) Training should be designed to impart an understanding of the alternative types of customer visiting the stand and the sales process to match those types – again described earlier in this book.

An exhibition should be part of an integrated marketing activities campaign with advertising, PR and direct contact marketing activities planned alongside both sequentially and concurrently.

Table 13.1 *Exhibition sales process*

Point in process	Objective	Practical steps
Just become aware of brand and concepts	Qualify, fact-find, build relationship Make offer open to the end of that day or the show – if you are first stand visited Send to competitors Ascertain buyer type – owner/buyer/runner	Open with non-threatening dialogue – with everyone Deliver evidence of six Cs Ask questions, qualify: if owner, test close; if runner, offer all literature
Aware but not a customer	A sales opportunity – test close	Deliver evidence of six Cs
Sales opportunity	Win sale	Find buyer needs Close sale
Customer	Demonstrate previously correct purchase occurred, show new items, close sale	Feedback on performance Keep in contact Contact plan Put across matched benefits

Tips

1. Choose your exhibition with care. Treat attendance figures with suspicion and investigate the provenance of those attending previous exhibitions. Exhibition organizers will stretch figures in creative ways. Sometimes the actual visitor types are not those you have been led to expect. A sport show in the height of the summer held at a prestigious venue unsurprisingly attracted few of the sports professionals said by the exhibition organizers to be attending; the

professionals were all out earning and they did not attend. The show was a flop for exhibitors.

2. Train direct selling and sales staff for the 21st-century customer environment. Training of direct selling staff is the biggest factor in increased turnover and gross profit. With one Helmsmen client, an increase in 22 per cent (on the bottom line at a stroke) was achieved through direct selling staff training. Where effective sales training is in place, the result is increased turnover and more profitable sales. Effectiveness is when the sales staff fully understand the buyer process and the sales process is developed to match, putting across the six Cs to the customer at the appropriate points in time. Many direct selling (or indeed sales) people have no understanding of either the buying process for the concept for sale (the product or service) or the sales process developed to match.

3. Sales and direct selling training is still often unrelated to the concept. It is given as a generic, using methods operated for decades, usually based on principles designed to sell what is made, ignoring the change and improvement in customer appreciation of choice, respect and need for human relations. It over-emphasizes the development of confidence, almost to the point of bullying and psyches people up to go for sales. Sales training is better in the franchise or chain catering sector (sandwich, fast food, snacks and branded restaurants), which requires training to be carried out in the franchise contract both for sales putting across the concept and brand need and to meet health and safety standards. As new products and services are introduced, then further training should be planned and implemented. Sales training should not just be a one-off activity but routinely injected as part of an organization's learning about the customer process and the preferred sales process matched to the buyer.

4. In an integrated marketing campaign, including salespeople carrying out sales calls, it may be easiest to ring fence the campaign so their part in securing orders can be measured and their improved contribution set against previous periods while the cost of all the contributing marketing activities is added to the cost of employing the salespeople themselves.

5. Salespeople need to be closely controlled. The damage that poor sales calls can generate cannot be overestimated and sales call performance should be monitored with the customer. Any personality clashes should be monitored and remedied by transferring customer responsibility to another salesperson. Salespeople's remuneration should be carefully calculated to be mutually beneficial to the salesperson and to the firm. Where they are not able to perform to match their targets set then, if any remedial training is unsuccessful, they should be released from their contract. When recruiting salespeople, great care should be taken to take up references and ensure they are genuine and positive.

6. Agent remuneration should be drawn up in a contract that is mutually beneficial, with targets set for performance in the long term and for an initial trial period, which are based on order-taking that matches the period of the year and the distribution potential. Setting a trial period is always helpful.

7. Names collected *ad hoc* at exhibitions (business cards in a hat) you should use only for awareness mailshots. Exhibition names are useful when a completed questionnaire giving some form of profile and qualifying information accompanies them.

8. Some salespeople have been known to extend the monies claimed beyond the true expenses owed. The reasons for such behaviour are often complex. It is important to bear in mind that the rules set are often considered fair game to optimize claims by salespeople. A salesperson who decides to leave a firm or is given notice may seek to optimize the salary/commission and expenses mix for their final period of employment by obtaining sales that less discerning clients accept and are then unable to sell on to their own customers or to use themselves, prior to the departure of the salesperson. Subsequent recriminations if not handled well can lead to an end to a customer relationship and even the customer ceasing to be a customer.

Accountability: setting and measuring key performance indicators

Sales figures from daily or weekly reconciliation will give the gross profit achievement. Comparison of variation of achievement achieved by different persons may give a clue as to the benefit of sales training but be aware of the different hours and days worked.

Clearly, the purpose of an exhibition stand will to an extent determine what should be measured. The aim may be to acquire a target number of orders for the concept, that is your products and services. The order-taking success may include those taken at the exhibition itself or include orders that can be attributed to the customer attending the exhibition but ordering subsequently. The purpose may be to elicit a target number of enquiries or a database of potential customers from exhibition visitors.

The successful achievement of the exhibition may be to make either a gross or a net profit from the exhibition – a positive figure arising for either orders less costs, or profit on orders less costs.

Participation in the exhibition may be a part of a brand value awareness exercise. In which case, a target of awareness improvement could be set.

Key performance indicator mechanisms

Measure the sales orders taken by day and time, by customer, by area. Measure trends. Compare with previous periods and previous years. Compare salespeople by area, by category and in comparison with other salespeople. Compare sales achievements with and without any other marketing activities within integrated marketing campaigns.

Salespeople, like any other staff, will have annual work objectives set and these should be appraised as normal. Measure the cost of marketing activity versus target. Measure the effect on profit. To measure an improvement in awareness resulting from an exhibition campaign activity a survey of your target market will need to be conducted before and after the exhibition. Measure sales over a period starting from before the sales training was introduced.

Use mystery shopper reports over a period of time to compare individual outlet's performance – measure performance and improvements. Compare between outlets. In the short term, use the successful outlets to understand how the poorer outlets could be improved rather than using the reports to chastise poor performers.

Exhibition attendance figures can be obtained from the organizers. Stand footfall can be measured with a visitor counter or using a box for business cards (with raffle prize?) or stapling cards to enquiry forms or writing down names and details of stand visitors and subsequently counting them. Order numbers and order values by customer resulting both at the exhibition and from subsequent marketing activity – as long as that activity is encompassed within the ring fence of the exhibition – should be reasonably readily obtained. Long-term customers resulting from initial contact at exhibitions can be measured as long as a field in the database indicates that the customer was acquired at the exhibition.

What costs will be involved in field marketing?

The cost of employing a salesperson should be considerably less than the business they bring in and the profit they generate. The hidden costs of employing salespeople should be included, such as supervision, processing claims, the cost of administration (converting an order into a completed sale). The Internet by comparison costs next to nothing.

To get a true picture of cost it is necessary to ring fence the marketing activities carefully. Training and staff costs for the exhibition should be added to the costs along with the supporting marketing activities such as direct mailing, advertising, PR, stand literature costs and the costs of the space, the stand and equipment as well.

Code of practice and the law

In addition to the DMA Code of Practice – see Chapter 4 – see also the 'DMA Best Practice Guidelines for Field Marketing' and 'The DMA User Guide to Field Marketing'. For further information on both, see Appendix 3.

Appendix 1: Measuring the effectiveness of this book

The author and the publisher, Kogan Page, would welcome feedback on this book. Feedback may take any number of forms – please write or e-mail roddywpmullin@hotmail.com. Please also answer our 10 questions given below.

The key measurement we would like to know from you is whether we have met this book's purpose? That is, have we provided you with what you need to carry out direct marketing? So please write or e-mail and let us know:

1. Are you now able to carry out or supervise direct marketing as a result of reading this book?
2. Did you find the book stimulating and as a bonus now go for direct marketing with enthusiasm?

We tried to provide in the first three chapters, sufficient background and understanding of marketing to deploy direct marketing successfully:

3. Did you feel the first three chapters provided enough background and understanding of marketing?

Chapters 4 to 13 each covered an aspect of direct marketing:

4. Was the content of each direct marketing chapter sufficient for you to carry out that activity? If not please elaborate on any shortfalls.
5. Was the chapter format helpful?
6. Are there any other activities peripheral to direct marketing activities that we should include? (Next time we may include warehouse sales, packaging.) Anything else?

Finally, we included in this book many suggestions for measuring marketing effectiveness for use by you, or for use by those responsible to you for marketing activity:

7. Did you or those responsible to you find the measurement mechanisms suggested useful?
8. What was the most useful measurement mechanism and why?
9. Did you use any other mechanisms? Please give details.
10. What have you done as a result?

We would appreciate any additional general comments you have.

Appendix 2: History, facts and figures about direct marketing

History

Direct marketing as a term was invented some time in the 1950s. Originally, it was seen as the door-to-door salesperson. Then for a number of years direct mail earned the title of 'junk mail' – usually with letters addressed to a 'Dear Sir or Madam'. The reason was that it was not always possible to be certain about the quality of the name and address list and it was expensive to personalize. Direct marketing has now grown to encompass all the areas that are the subject of this book.

Direct marketing was never really expected to produce sales as a result of a single activity. Rather it was seen as establishing a dialogue to achieve a position on the prospect's mental shopping list. Relationship-building to encourage loyalty was seen as a second purpose. Described for many years as 'below the line' advertising, direct marketing was seen as a kind of poor relation to the above-the-line of display, TV and cinema advertising. Advertising became over-creative for a time, producing material for which no sales results could be seen and in the mid-1990s, the move to the more readily accountable direct marketing started and has grown ever since.

Technology has undoubtedly helped achieve growth. The ability to mail merge a database with a blank letter started in the 1980s but really only became widespread in the 1990s. The arrival of the Internet in the 1990s brought in a new direct marketing tool – the e-mail. This went through years of boom and bust at the end of the 1990s before the coming of a second age of the Internet, starting in 2001.

Telemarketing, the outbound call centre service, was joined by an inbound service. Call centres sprung up everywhere – initially provided by specialist firms but later being set up in-house to answer calls from direct response TV and to man customer service centres.

Direct response TV meant displaying a telephone number of a call centre on the advertisement with a team of people ready to handle the rush of calls after advertisement showings on TV or routinely for magazine responses. Then the Internet arrived and the call centre number was joined by a Web site address. Now interactive TV is supplementing the capability, from a start really only in 2000. This allows a person to move from their digital TV to the Internet at the press of a button from where they can order.

Finally joining the new media has been text messaging using the mobile phone, also known as the mobile Internet. This has really only been developed as an advertising media in 2001. It is a permission-based operation. It grew as a result of the phenomenal level of text messaging being carried out.

Catalogue sales arose out of the need in the USA to buy articles, other than commodities that were often the only items available in local shops, due to the spread of the population. Catalogues were very large, containing a huge range of items. In the UK, the advent of easy credit in the 1930s meant that payments for goods could be spread over an agreed period of time. Purchasing from catalogues became the norm for the working class of those times where disposable incomes were small.

Catalogues were taken round to homes by an agent, who also took orders and then collected payments. This was rewarded with commission. Now the business has shifted away from the use of agents. Catalogues are sent to individuals rather than being agent-based. The link with the working class has been difficult to remove. Catalogue sales are still valued as a discreet way of obtaining credit. However the advent of the general acceptability of credit cards means this is less relevant. The emphasis is now on the goods that are available.

Facts

Direct mail (source: DMIS)

- 4,664 million items were mailed in 2000.
- These were split between 75 per cent (3,516 million) consumer mailings and 25 per cent (1,448 million) business mailings.
- The overall volume of direct mail has increased by over 100 per cent in the last 10 years.
- £2,049 million was spent on direct mail in 2000.
- Direct mail expenditure has increased by 120 per cent in the last 10 years.
- Direct mail expenditure in 2000 is split between postage at £89 million and production at £1,480 million.
- It is estimated that consumer direct mail generates more than £20 billion worth of business every year.

Receipt and treatment

- The average household receives 12–14 items of mail every four weeks.
- Business managers receive an average of 14 items per week at work.
- 75 per cent of consumer direct mail is opened, 53 per cent is opened and read, 26 per cent is kept to be read later or passed on to somebody else.
- Business managers open 83 per cent, 9 per cent is re-directed to a colleague and 16 per cent is filed or responded to.
- AB households receive considerably more direct Mail than the average UK household (an average of 207 items per annum) does.
- Overall, 62 per cent of direct mail is requested by consumers.
- The average consumer spends approximately £440 through direct mail per year.

Satisfaction and acceptance

■ 86 per cent of consumers are either 'very' or 'quite' satisfied with the products they buy through direct mail.

■ 49 per cent of business people consider direct mail a 'useful' or 'quite useful' source of information.

■ 56 per cent of consumers said that convenience was the main benefit of buying through direct mail whilst 58 per cent said value for money.

■ 62 per cent of consumers like to receive special offers or money-off vouchers through the post.

■ 85 per cent of consumers accept that companies with whom they trade should mail them when they have a special offer (58 per cent), a new product or service (50 per cent) or a new catalogue or brochure (55 per cent).

Use and users of direct mail

■ One-third of total advertising expenditure is spent on direct mail in the top 3,000 companies who have someone responsible for direct mail.

■ 61 per cent of direct mail users and potential users claimed direct mail would become more important in the next five years.

■ The main decision on which advertising media to use is taken by the Marketing Director (36 per cent) and the Managing Director (30 per cent).

Figures

See Chapter 1 for a table and figures on the size of direct marketing with respect to all other marketing. The tables and figures below are included to give a better feel for direct marketing. The author is grateful for the permission given to publish them here. The DMA Census of the Direct Marketing Industry should be consulted if further information is sought. It provides a quantitative and qualitative review and analysis of the UK Direct Marketing Industry.

Table A.1 *Total advertising expenditure 1990–2000 (£millions)*

	Press	TV	Outdoor & Transport	Radio	Cinema	Direct Mail	Internet	Total
1989	5131	2288	271	159	35	758	–	8642
1990	5137	2325	282	163	39	930	–	8876
1991	4884	2295	267	149	42	895	–	8532
1992	4957	2472	284	157	45	945	–	8860
1993	5085	2604	300	194	49	904	–	9136
1994	5552	2888	350	243	53	1050	–	10136
1995	5979	3136	411	296	69	1135	–	11026
1996	6413	3379	466	344	73	1404	–	12079
1997	6967	3704	545	393	88	1635	8	13340
1998	7531	4029	613	460	97	1665	19	14414
1999	7877	4320	649	516	123	1876	51	15412
2000	8609	4646	823	595	128	2049	155	17005

Source: AA/DMIS

Share of total expenditure in 2000

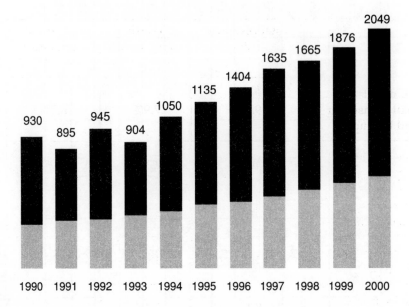

Figure A.1 *Direct mail expenditure 1990–2000 (£millions)*

Table A.2 *Direct mail response rates*

	Total response rate	Excluding campaigns over 50%	Excluding campaigns over 30%
All direct mail (consumer and business)	9.6%	7.9%	6.5%
Base (number of campaigns)	1053	1015	970
All consumer direct mail	10%	8.3%	6.8%
Base (number of campaigns)	1053	1015	970
All business direct mail	9.1%	7.4%	6.2%
Base (number of campaigns)	806	718	750
Door-to-door	7.8%	6.1%	2.8%
Base (number of campaigns)	212	205	187

Source: DMIS Response Rates Survey, 2000

Table A.3 *Response rates by sector*

%	Total	Excluding campaigns over 50%	Excluding campaigns over 30%
Base number of campaigns	1053	1015	970
All direct mail (response rate)	9.6	7.9	6.5
All consumer direct mail (response rate)	10	8.3	6.8
Consumer services	19.5	11.2	7,.2
Consumer research	27.5	13.8	13.8
Furnishing	7.2	7.2	4.3
Food and drink	17.9	13.3	11
Automotive	11.7	10.7	8.2
Entertainment/leisure	11.1	10.5	8.5
Retail	12.6	12.6	6.9
Travel – consumer	10.6	9.8	7.9
Gardening	13.1	13.1	11.8
Charity/donation	9.4	9.4	7.9
Property/consumer	12.6	6.6	6.6
DIY	1.9	1.9	1.9
Household goods and toiletries	8	8	6
Utilities	7	7	7
Brown goods – TV hi-fi, radio etc	22.6	11.8	11.8
White goods – fridges, washers etc	6.1	6.1	6.1

Table A.3 *(cont'd)*

Magazines & newspapers	8.5	8.5	5.9
Books, music, video	5	5	5
Clothing	9.8	9.8	8.7
Big 5 mail order	12	19.2	8
Collectables	5.4	5.4	5.4
Telecomms & mobile phones	4.2	4.2	4.2
Computer software and hardware	11.4	6	6
Financial – insurance	5.3	5.3	5.3
Financial – investment	4.7	3.5	3.5
Financial – credit cards	3.5	3.5	3.5
Financial – banks and building societies	8.1	5.2	5.2
Financial – other	3.3	3.3	3.3
Information/newsletter	10.7	8.3	6.5
Gift/gifting service	10.6	6.4	6.4
Luxury goods	4.1	4.1	4.1
Health products	12.6	9.4	9.4
Membership renewal promotion	15.5	12.3	7.8
Personal loans	3	3	3
Mortgages	15	15	2.1
Tobacco	13.9	13.9	13.9

Source: DMIS Response Rates Survey, 2000

Table A.4 *Direct mail costs example for 5,000 mail shot*

Element	Description	Cost
Outer envelope (C5 – fits A5 size)	Headline printed on front in 1 colour with logo in 1 colour on reverse	£525
Letterhead	A4 letterhead with 4 colour logo	£480
Small brochure (A4 to be folded into 4 page A5)	Both sides printed in 4 colours throughout including 1 minimum size transparency and a logo	£950
Larger brochure (A4)	A4 8 page brochure, 4 colour throughout, 1 full page scan, 6 medium size scans	£1,490
List broking services	*Normally rate at a cost per 100. Discounts can be given if volumes are large	£215
Lasering and enclosing services	Enclosing + sealing of brochures into A5 window envelope. Softing and mailing	£340

Source: Royal Mail

Table A.5 *Opening and reading of direct mail by filterers and managers*

%	Filterers	Managers
Opened	83	76
Treatment of opened direct mail by filterers		
Pass straight to manager	20	
Pass elsewhere	8	
Look at and pass to manager	24	
Look at and file	3	
Look at and throw away	28	
Treatment of opened direct mail by managers		
Look at and throw away	56	
Look at and file	13	
Pass elsewhere	9	
Respond/consider responding	3	

Source: DMIS Business to Business Direct Mail Trends Survey, 2000

Table A.6 *Opening and reading of direct mail by sector*

%	Opened and read (all or most items)
Automotive (manufacturer)	72
Automotive (car dealers)	71
Food and drink	81
Household appliances (TVs)	59
Household appliances (CD-hi-fis)	57
Household appliances (washing machines)	64
Household goods and toiletries	63
Home shopping	84
Insurance (life)	47
Insurance (motor)	58
Insurance (home contents)	16
Insurance (buildings)	16
Leisure	79
Publishing	75
Retail (supermarket)	78
Retail (department store)	56
Retail (fashion)	67
Travel (travel agent)	85
Travel (UK package holiday company)	74
Travel (tourist board)	87
Savings and investments	70

Source: DMIS Sector Intelligence Surveys, base sizes varied

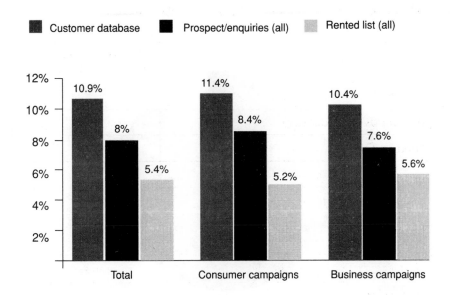

Figure A.2 *Response rate according to list type*

Source: DMIS Response Rate Survey, 2000

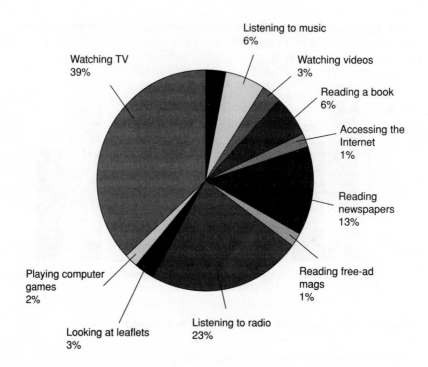

Source: Newspaper Society, CCIV

Base 2014: All media consumed Monday to Friday

Figure A.3 *Share of media time (Monday to Friday)*

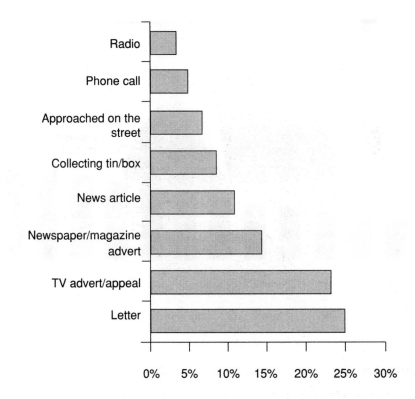

Figure A.4 *How have you heard about various charities?*

Source: Future Foundations, Charity Awareness Monitor, 1990/00

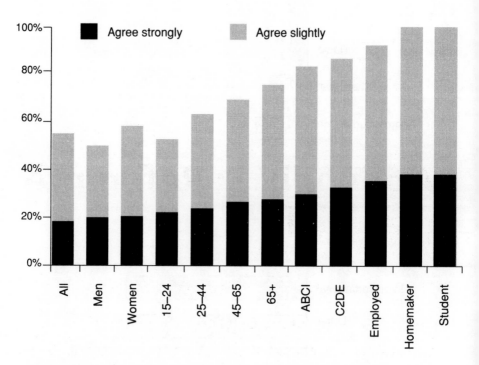

Figure A.5 *I don't like buying items without seeing them first – UK*

Source: DMA/Future Foundation: Responding to the Future, 2000

Appendix 3: Reference material

BOOKS

General marketing books

A useful quick practical book on marketing is:

Davey, R and Jacks, A (2000) *How to be Better at Marketing*, Kogan Page, London

A valuable book that is also practical and gives inexpensive ideas for marketing:

Forsyth, P (2000) *Marketing on a Tight Budget*, Kogan Page, London

The written equivalent of a Web site's 'frequently asked questions':

Smith, P (1999) *Great Answers to Tough Marketing Questions*, Kogan Page, London

For general creative help:

Yadin, D (2001) *Creative Marketing Communications*, Kogan Page, London

And for appropriate marketing communications:

Smith, PR, Berry, C and Pulford, A (1999) *Strategic Marketing Communications*, Kogan Page, London

Measuring marketing books

Mullin, R (2001) *Value for Money Marketing*, Kogan Page, London
Shaw, R (1998) *Improving marketing effectiveness*, The Economist Books, London

Direct marketing

For a lovely readable book:

Bird, D (2000) *Commonsense Direct Marketing*, 4th edn, Kogan Page, London

Bird, D (1996) *How to Write Letters that Sell*, Kogan Page, London

As an essential guide for beginners this book covers direct mail, direct response advertising, door-to-door, piggy backs, telemarketing, the Internet, catalogues:

Donovan, J (2000) *DIY Direct Marketing*, Kogan Page, London

Advertising

Davis, M P (1997) *Successful Advertising*, Cassell, London

Market research

The best book the author has found on market research (obtain a copy):

Birn, R (2000) *The Handbook of International Market Research*, Kogan Page, London

Competition

A guide to analysing your competition's performance:

Fisher, J *How to Beat Your Competitors*, Kogan Page, London

Agencies

A book covering advertising, sales promotion, market research agencies, PR, direct mail and marketing consultants, exhibition services. This book is full of useful contacts:

Smith, G (1994) *Getting the Best from Agencies*, Kogan Page, London

USEFUL FIRMS

Extranets, Intranets, the Internet

www.Marketingnet.com (also their book: Bickerton, P, Bickerton, M and Simpson-Holley (1998) *Cyberstrategy*, Butterworth-Heinemann, Oxford

e-business/CRM

Informatica
www.informatica.com

Customer profiles/lists

CACI Limited
CACI House
Kensington Village
Avonmore Road
London W14 8TS
Tel: (0207) 602 6000
e-mail: marketing@caci.co.uk

CCN/Mosaic
39 Houndsditch Road
London EC3A 5DB
Tel: (0207) 623 5551

CDMS/Superprofiles
Kershaw Avenue
Crosby
Liverpool L23 0XA

Equifax/Define
Capital House
25 Shapel Street
London NW1 5DS

ICD Marketing Services Ltd
Boundary House
91–93 Charterhouse Street
London EC1M 6HR

Mobile Internet

www.airmedia.co.uk
www.nightfly.co.uk
www.distractions.co.com This site has a fantastic beat and a chance to play with a WAP phone.

Interactive TV

Open... +44 (0)20 7332 7000/(0)870 60 60 60 4 – the Web site is barred unless you have Sky digital.

Fulfilment

www.grange-direct.co.uk – Jenny Moseley is the expert on Mailsort and is the present DMA Chairperson.

Web site-based directories

Seek (0800 169 6820) (www.seekdirectory.co.uk)

Web site, CD ROM, DVD, video design

Concise
Unit 32, Pall Mall Deposit
124 Barlby Road
London W10 6BL
Tel: (020) 8964 4446
www.concisegroup.com

Send/call/ask for a free copy of their demo disk:

DVA
8 Campbell Court
Bramley
Tadley
Hampshire RG26 5EG
Tel: (01256) 882032
www.dva.co.uk

Call centres

BPS Teleperformance
Albany House
Hurst Street
Birmingham B5 4BD
Tel: (0121) 666 6161
www.teleperformance.com

Telephone surveys, omnibus surveys

Telephone Thursdays – results Monday

MORI Telephone Surveys
Parchment House
13 Northburgh Street
London EC1V 0JP
Tel: (020) 7490 5800
www.moritel.co.uk

AUTHORITIES

Data protection

Data Protection Registrar
Wycliffe House
Water Lane
Wilmslow
Cheshire SK9 5AF
Tel: (01625) 545700
Data protection Web sites
www.dataprotection.gov.uk/
www.ccta.gov.uk/dpr/dpdoc.nsf
www.dpr.gov.uk/
www.hmso.gov.uk/acts1998/19980029.htm
www.acs.ohio-state.edu/units/law/swire1/psecind.htm
www.truste.org/

Regulatory bodies

The EU Distance Selling Regulations – see Institute of Sales Promotion Web site – www.isp.org.uk

Advertising Standards Authority
Brook House
2–16 Torrington Place
London WC1E 7HN
Tel: (0207) 580 5555

ITC
31 Foley Street
London W1
Tel: (0207) 255 3000

ASSOCIATIONS

CMT
Causeway House
The Causeway
Teddington
Middlesex TW11 0JR

Direct Mail Information Service
5 Carlisle Street
London W1V 5RG
Tel: (0207) 494 0483
http://www.dmis.co.uk/keystats/facts.htm

DMA Door-to-Door Council (formerly Association of Household Distributors Limited) – see DMA address below.

For Code of Practice, Who's who in direct marketing, Insert guide, Field marketing guides, etc:

Direct Marketing Association
DMA House
70 Margaret Street
London W1W 8SP
Tel: (0207) 291 3300
www.dma.org.uk

Institute of Direct Marketing
1 Park Road
Teddington
Middlesex TW11 0AR

Mailing Preference Service
5 Reef House
Plantation Wharf
London SW11 3UF

Mail Order Protection Scheme
16 Took's Court
London EC3 1LB

Market Research Society
15 Northburgh Street
London EC1V 0AH

NDL
Port House
Square Rigger Road
Plantation Wharf
London SW11 3TY

Print and Publishers Association
Queens House
28 Kingsway
London WC2B 6JR

Royal Mail
Tel: (08457) 950950
www.royalmail.com

Telephone Preference Service
6 Reef House
Plantation Wharf
London SW11 3UF

Marketing training

The Chartered Institute of Marketing (CIM) runs many courses designed to train anybody from any discipline in the appropriate part of marketing for the task in hand – 0 (044) 1628 427200 for CIM training (www.cim.co.uk)

Index